Harvest the Fruit
of the
Spirit

Weekly Spiritual Growth

DUSTIN BEENKEN

WESTBOW
P R E S S®
A DIVISION OF THOMAS NELSON
& ZONDERVAN

WestBow Press books may be ordered through booksellers or by contacting:

WestBow Press
A Division of Thomas Nelson & Zondervan
1663 Liberty Drive
Bloomington, IN 47403
www.westbowpress.com
1 (866) 928-1240

ISBN: 978-1-4908-8614-5 (sc)
ISBN: 978-1-4908-8615-2 (hc)
ISBN: 978-1-4908-8613-8 (e)

Library of Congress Control Number: 2015910107

Print information available on the last page.

WestBow Press rev. date: 08/05/2015

But the fruit of the Spirit is love, joy, peace, patience, kindness, goodness, faithfulness, gentleness, self-control; against such things there is no law. GALATIANS 5:22–23

The moment we accept Jesus Christ into our lives, we are transformed. Our lives will never be the same. The Holy Spirit immediately becomes a part of us. The Holy Spirit directs our thoughts, actions, and lives so that we become more like Christ. We receive the fruit of the Spirit, nine attributes that define our lives as Christians. As we strengthen our Christian beliefs, the fruit of the Spirit grows within us. We will never completely overcome our sinful nature as human beings. However, as the fruit of the Spirit multiplies, we are able to overcome more of our sinful desires and live the life God intends for us.

Week 1: Love

For God so loved the world, that he gave his only Son, that whoever believes in him should not perish but have eternal life. For God did not send his Son into the world to condemn the world, but in order that the world might be saved through him.
JOHN 3:16–17

John 3:16 is one of the better-known verses of the Bible—and for good reason. It describes the entire truth of the Christian faith in one sentence. As a child attending Sunday school, this was the first verse that I memorized. I assume that this is the case for many of you as well.

God so loved the world: The first thing that we need to realize is that God loves us. God created each of us in His image. He made us unique with gifts and talents that we should use to further His Kingdom. As our Creator, He loves us with a love that we cannot fully comprehend. We love our spouses, children, siblings, other family members, and friends, but our love does not compare to the way that God loves us. God has perfect love for us. He loves us despite our faults and sinful nature. Through His grace, we have the gift of eternal life, if we chose to accept it.

He gave His only Son: God sent His Son, Jesus Christ, to be born of the Virgin Mary in Bethlehem. He came into this world as a vulnerable baby born in a lowly stable. Jesus lived in this world as a human and experienced life very similar to us. He faced obstacles, challenges, sorrows, and doubts. He also experienced joy, happiness, and laughter. Jesus was different from us in one major way. He was the Son of God and was free from sin. We have all sinned and fallen short of the glory of God. God made the ultimate sacrifice for His creation when Jesus was crucified for the forgiveness of our sins.

Whoever believes in Him should not perish but have eternal life: There is only one way to spend eternity with our Creator in Heaven. We must accept Jesus Christ as the Son of God and ask Him to be the leader of our lives. Jesus is our Lord and Savior. Through the grace of God and the gift of His Son, we can experience the wonders of Heaven. In Heaven there is no sickness, pain, or suffering. There is constant joy, happiness, peace, and love. We will forever worship and praise our God.

HARVEST THE FRUIT: Focus on the fact God always loves you. He is your biggest supporter. You are a precious child of God that He created in His image. If you have not accepted Jesus Christ as your Lord and Savior, make that commitment now. If you have already accepted Jesus into your life, reconfirm your faith. Dedicate yourself to living a life that shares the love and light of Jesus Christ with everyone you meet.

Week 2: Joy

Make a joyful noise to the Lord, all the earth! Serve the Lord with gladness! Come into his presence with singing! Know that the Lord, he is God! It is he who made us, and we are his; we are his people, and the sheep of his pasture. Enter his gates with thanksgiving, and his courts with praise! Give thanks to him; bless his name! For the Lord is good; his steadfast love endures forever, and his faithfulness to all generations. PSALM 100:1–5

We have so many things to be thankful and joyful about. Through the death and resurrection of Jesus Christ, we have been given the gift of everlasting life. We know that once our time on earth has ended we have a permanent home. A place where there is no worrying, sadness, sickness, or death. We will have perfect peace and contentment.

Until God calls us home, we need to make the most of our lives and live them to the best of our abilities. We only have a limited amount of time. We need to make the most of it. Too often Christians are viewed by others as seeing the negatives in the world. We will spend eternity in Heaven, but with all of the pain and suffering in this world, it is hard to keep an optimistic and positive attitude. Part of our responsibility as Christians is to witness to others and help lead them to Christ. If we are seen as being negative or constantly pessimistic, what kind of example are we showing? It does not show others the joy, hope, and peace that we have received through Jesus Christ. This life is too short to dwell on the negative things. We need to focus on all of the beauty and wonderful things that God has created. Having a positive outlook makes our lives more enjoyable. It is also a great way to be a witness for God. Others will see the joy we have for life and for the Lord. Our actions and attitudes can help lead others to accept Jesus Christ as their Savior.

One way that helps me keep a positive outlook is listening to and singing along with Christian music. Every voice, no matter what it sounds like, is pleasing to God when it is praising Him. There are so many inspirational songs that speak of God's love for us and the joy He brings to our lives. Music is a very powerful tool. When music is about Jesus Christ, it becomes significantly more powerful. It can dramatically change a person's life.

HARVEST THE FRUIT: Make a commitment for you and your family to listen to Christian music. Find a Christian radio station or buy a Christian CD. As you listen to the inspirational lyrics in the songs, try to incorporate the messages of joy, hope, peace, and love into your life. The lyrics are uplifting, and music is a great way to walk closer to God. If you carefully and thoughtfully listen to the messages, you will not be disappointed. Your life will change for the better.

Week 3: Peace

Jesus answered him, "If anyone loves me, he will keep my word, and my Father will love him, and we will come to him and make our home with him. Whoever does not love me does not keep my words. And the word that you hear is not mine but the Father's who sent me. These things I have spoken to you while I am still with you. But the Helper, the Holy Spirit, whom the Father will send in my name, he will teach you all things and bring to your remembrance all that I have said to you. Peace I leave with you; my peace I give to you. Not as the world gives do I give to you. Let not your hearts be troubled, neither let them be afraid."
JOHN 14:23–27

Jesus knew that His life was nearing the end. He was preparing Himself and the disciples for His impending death on the cross. The disciples do not fully understand what is going to happen. One of them will betray Jesus, one of them will deny Jesus three times, and their own lives will be endangered. Jesus reassures the disciples that He will not leave them alone after His death. His Father will provide them with a new Helper who will never leave or forsake them.

The Holy Spirit was sent to us by the Father in the name of His Son to further our understanding of God and continue the ministry of Jesus Christ. The Trinity: Father, Son, and Holy Spirit. One God that exists as three different beings. The Father who created the universe and everything in it. The Son who was sent to this world in human form to save us from our sins. The Holy Spirit who dwells in everyone who accepts Jesus Christ. It is a hard concept for us to understand, but it is an integral part of our Christian faith.

We will never totally grasp the awesomeness and wonders of our God as human beings. We see all things as temporary and within a limited set of parameters. Our finite, human intellectual capacity will never be able to fully understand the fact that we have one God who is the Father, the Son, and the Holy Spirit. Our infinite God knows this. He is our Creator and does not want us to fully understand everything. This is where faith comes in. We simply have to believe in that which we cannot see or completely understand and give our lives to Christ. Only then will we experience the true peace that Jesus promises.

HARVEST THE FRUIT: Think about how the Holy Spirit has worked in your life. It may have came in the form of a feeling directing you to do something, receiving a kind and encouraging word from a stranger, the lyrics in a Christian song that spoke to you, or the words in a sermon that seemed to be describing exactly what you were going through. God works in mysterious ways. If we take the time to listen carefully, He speaks to us through the Holy Spirit. He provides us with the peace we all long for. Think about a way the Holy Spirit can work through you to positively impact others.

Week 4: Patience

The Lord is not slow to fulfill his promise as some count slowness, but is patient toward you, not wishing that any should perish, but that all should reach repentance. But the day of the Lord will come like a thief, and then the heavens will pass away with a roar, and the heavenly bodies will be burned up and dissolved, and the earth and the works that are done on it will be exposed. But according to his promise we are waiting for new heavens and a new earth in which righteousness dwells. Therefore, beloved, since you are waiting for these, be diligent to be found by him without spot or blemish, and at peace. And count the patience of our Lord as salvation, just as our beloved brother Paul also wrote to you according to the wisdom given him. 2 PETER 3:9–10, 13–15

Everything happens according to God's will and on His schedule. Only God knows when the day of the Lord will come, the time when we will be called to our heavenly home. The only thing that we know for certain is the day will come, and it is closer today than it was yesterday. God is patient. He is waiting until all of His creation has heard about the salvation offered through His Son. Everyone deserves to hear about Jesus Christ and to be given the opportunity to accept Him as their Savior. We have a responsibility to share the hope we have been given through Jesus with everyone we meet.

Our lives on earth are short and unpredictable. This world and the things of this world will not last forever. We should strive to live righteous lives as Jesus taught, putting the needs of others before our own. We need to be prepared for when our time on this earth ends.

We have a responsibility to live each day as if it were our last. We must be ready for when we are called home. When that day comes, it will be too late if we have not accepted the salvation offered by Jesus Christ. It is the most important gift that we will ever be given.

We like to be in control of every aspect of our lives, but there are many things that we have no control over. What we can control is how we choose to live. Through the grace of God, we can also be in charge of where we go once this life is over. By living Christ-centered lives and sharing the love we receive from God, we also have the opportunity to positively influence where others spend eternity. Make an effort to lead others to Christ; they will be forever changed.

HARVEST THE FRUIT: Be thankful that our God is patient, but realize that our time on earth could end at anytime. Have you accepted the salvation that we have been given through Jesus Christ? Have a discussion with your loved ones about your faith and what accepting Jesus Christ as your Savior has meant to you. Ask your loved ones to share their faith story. Encourage and pray for others to make the life-changing decision to follow Jesus, if they have not yet accepted the salvation offered through the grace of God.

Week 5: Kindness

Note then the kindness and the severity of God: severity toward those who have fallen, but God's kindness to you, provided you continue in his kindness. Otherwise you too will be cut off. And even they, if they do not continue in their unbelief, will be grafted in, for God has the power to graft them in again. For if you were cut from what is by nature a wild olive tree, and grafted, contrary to nature, into a cultivated olive tree, how much more will these, the natural branches, be grafted back into their own olive tree. ROMANS 11:22–24

God is our ultimate judge. We will all be judged by Him when the time comes. If we have not accepted Jesus Christ into our lives, the punishment will be severe. If we have accepted Jesus, the reward that we receive will be unparalleled. We need to be diligent and faithful in living the way God has commanded. We should continually strive to get a better understanding of God and our Christian faith. We have a responsibility to grow our relationship with God by thoroughly reading and studying the Bible, attending church regularly, and dedicating every aspect of our lives to Christ.

In the gospel of John, chapter 15, Jesus tells us He is the Vine, His Father is the Vinedresser, and we are the branches. The Father tends and cares for the fruitful branches to make them more productive, but He removes the unfruitful branches. The unfruitful branches wither and are thrown into the fire. Fortunately, we have a kind and forgiving God. According to this week's Scripture reading, unfruitful branches can be grafted back into the Vine, if they repent and ask Jesus Christ to lead their lives. We are one with God, through Christ, who makes all things possible. Without Him, we are lost.

It is reassuring to know that God considers us a part of Him. He wants us to be happy and live our lives with purpose. His love and kindness are always surrounding us. They are endless. We are His masterpiece. Even though we are imperfect, He will never leave us. We are unclean and uncultivated, but through the sacrifice of Jesus Christ, we are made pure. His body was broken and His blood was spilled to cleanse us of our sins. Jesus overcame the grave, so we too can overcome death.

HARVEST THE FRUIT: Thank God for the kindness and patience He shows us. Read John 15 along with this week's reading and focus on living a life that produces abundant fruit. Have you or someone you know drifted away from God? There is no better time than now to rededicate your life to Him. Make a commitment to help others live fruitful and abundant lives through Jesus Christ.

Week 6: Goodness

The Lord is my shepherd; I shall not want. He makes me lie down in green pastures. He leads me beside still waters. He restores my soul. He leads me in paths of righteousness for his name's sake. Even though I walk through the valley of the shadow of death, I will fear no evil, for you are with me; your rod and your staff, they comfort me. You prepare a table before me in the presence of my enemies; you anoint my head with oil; my cup overflows. Surely goodness and mercy shall follow me all the days of my life, and I shall dwell in the house of the Lord forever. PSALM 23:1–6

A shepherd is constantly caring for his flock. His job never ends. He directs the flock where to go. He leads them to food and water. He protects them from any dangers they incur. He is willing to put himself in harm's way to make sure that his flock is safe. If a sheep is lost, he searches for the sheep and brings it back to the others. The shepherd does everything he can to ensure his flock fulfills their purpose. The flock is completely dependent on their shepherd. Without the shepherd, the flock would be in complete disarray.

The Lord is the Good Shepherd. We are His sheep. God is always present, protecting us and directing us through life. God's goodness, kindness, and mercy toward us are without fail. God protects us. He calls us back to Him when we lose our way in life. He is there for us in the good times as well as the bad. God rejoices with us in our successes and suffers with us in our failures. He is there to comfort us in our times of need. There is no limit to what God will do for us or what we can do through Him.

We must always remember that God loves us and wants us to be happy. True joy can only come through a personal relationship with Jesus Christ. We have been given a multitude of blessings in our lives. We should place our focus on the many blessings we have received instead of dwelling on the things that we think we are missing out on. There will always be someone with more than us, but we truly have everything we need through the goodness of God. There will be times when we feel like we are alone and that the world is against us. It is during those times that we need to rely on God the most. His divine goodness can always be found. He is always there and is only a prayer away.

HARVEST THE FRUIT: Focus on all of the great things God has done for you. God has blessed each of us in numerous ways. Thank Him for the life He has given you. Discuss a difficult time that you had during your life. How did God comfort you and help you out of the valley? Thank God for the direction He provided. Be thankful for the people in your life and make sure that they know you appreciate them.

Week 7: Faithfulness

Let the heavens praise your wonders, O Lord, your faithfulness in the assembly of the holy ones! For who in the skies can be compared to the Lord? Who among the heavenly beings is like the Lord, a God greatly to be feared in the council of the holy ones, and awesome above all who are around him? O Lord God of hosts, who is mighty as you are, O Lord, with your faithfulness all around you? You rule the raging of the sea; when its waves rise, you still them. Righteousness and justice are the foundation of your throne; steadfast love and faithfulness go before you.
PSALM 89:5–9, 14

Great is the Lord's faithfulness. Our God is deserving of all of our praise. He is our Creator and Redeemer. Through Him, we are made complete. God is greater than everything in this world. We are not worthy of His mighty power. His wonders and mercy are beyond compare. God is in complete control of all things. He directs the vastness of the universe and everything in it. He rules the earth and all of His creation. He knows our deepest desires and needs. God is righteous, honorable, and just. His love and devotion will never end.

We tend to idolize the wrong things in life. We admire celebrities, athletes, or the rich and famous. God has blessed them with talents that allow them to do great things based on our human barometer. We should always remember that the people we revere in life are no different from anyone else in the eyes of God. We are all His children and deserve to be respected and loved. God has provided talents and gifts to all of us which should be used in His name. We can all do extraordinary things in our lives. We may not become rich or famous, but we can have a lasting impact on the lives of others.

We are blessed to have a faithful and loving God. Our Lord is true to His word. He will never leave our side. We can take comfort in the fact that He is constantly reliable and loyal to all of His people. Everything we have been given comes from God according to His master plan. We need to place our complete trust in Him in every situation we face. We will not always understand why things happen, but we can trust that it is according to His will. We can never lose faith that He will be there for us no matter what we are going through. How great is God's faithfulness!

HARVEST THE FRUIT: Focus on the faithfulness of our God. God has given us everything in our lives according to His plan. His mercy and love are never-ending. Thank God for the blessings He has given you. Discuss with your family the different ways God has been faithful to you in your life. It is all right to admire our heroes in life, but worship God alone. Use your God-given gifts to do extraordinary things.

Week 8: Gentleness

For you are my lamp, O Lord, and my God lightens my darkness. For by you I can run against a troop, and by my God I can leap over a wall. This God—his way is perfect; the word of the Lord proves true; he is a shield for all those who take refuge in him. For who is God, but the Lord? And who is a rock, except our God? This God is my strong refuge and has made my way blameless. He made my feet like the feet of a deer and set me secure on the heights. He trains my hands for war, so that my arms can bend a bow of bronze. You have given me the shield of your salvation, and your gentleness made me great. 2 SAMUEL 22:29–36

All things are possible with God. We can accomplish anything through Him. Nothing is beyond the mighty power of our Creator. He protects those who seek refuge. He strengthens those who are weak. He provides light in the darkness. He grants salvation to everyone who believes in Him. He is the Almighty to be feared and revered. His gentle hand comforts us in our times of need. He is the rock that we can build our lives upon. God was with us yesterday, He is with us today, and He will be with us tomorrow.

We have all experienced times when we feel hopeless or that something is impossible. Never forget that God has given us the shield of His salvation. He will protect us at all costs. He has paid the price for our sins. He has given us the gift of eternal life through Jesus Christ. Our destination has been determined. We should celebrate our lives on earth knowing that through our acceptance of

Jesus Christ we will never die. We can never forget the hope that we have received from God.

We will never come close to reaching the perfection of God. We have all sinned and will continue to have transgressions during our lives. Thankfully, the Lord's gentleness makes all of us great. God is caring and not self-serving. He is slow to anger and quick to forgive. God is supremely limitless. Only He completely knows what is the best for us. We need to submit to God and let Him be in control of our lives. When we live our lives for God instead of ourselves, we will experience a feeling of freedom like never before. As John the Baptist said, "Jesus must increase, but I must decrease."

HARVEST THE FRUIT: Focus on the gentleness God has shown you. Thank Him for the comfort and reassurance He has given. He has provided us with everything we will ever need. Through the acceptance of His Son, we are guaranteed eternal life. Because of His sacrifice we always have hope. Discuss the gentleness you have experienced from God in your life. Ask God to help you share His gentleness with everyone you meet.

Week 9: Self-Control

For this very reason, make every effort to supplement your faith with virtue, and virtue with knowledge, and knowledge with self-control, and self-control with steadfastness, and steadfastness with godliness, and godliness with brotherly affection, and brotherly affection with love. For if these qualities are yours and are increasing, they keep you from being ineffective or unfruitful in the knowledge of our Lord Jesus Christ. 2 PETER 1:5–8

We should constantly strive to grow closer to God. We need to be disciplined to reach our full potential as both human beings and Christians. Through studying the Bible, we gain a better understanding of our God and the type of life that He calls us to live. We should regularly attend church with our families and have fellowship with other Christians. By dedicating ourselves to being morally good in all that we do, we can be an example for others to follow. We should seek to have complete control over our thoughts, words, and actions. We are called to have unwavering loyalty to God and the people in our lives. Most importantly, we need to have a profound love for God, others, and ourselves.

We are never finished becoming the person God wants us to be. We need to have a strong foundation in Christ. We must be planted in the good soil that only comes from knowing God, so we can continue to grow as Christians. We must be firmly rooted in our core Christian beliefs. With a strong foundation and solid roots, we are then able to grow into the person that God created us to be. Once we are planted firmly in Christ, we can then help lead others to salvation. It won't always be easy or comfortable, but if we continue to grow and live as Christ lived, our spiritual reward will be beyond our comprehension.

We have been given everything that we need to live abundant lives. We have a Father who created and loves us. We have a Son who died for our sins so that we may live. We have a Holy Spirit that is always with us. The Bible provides a perfect blueprint for us to base our lives on. We should always strive to live as Jesus taught. With self-control and discipline, we can grow spiritually and make a meaningful difference in the lives of everyone we encounter. We can do amazing things when we submit completely to God.

HARVEST THE FRUIT: Focus on disciplining yourself to continually grow your relationship with God. Make sure that you have a strong foundation planted in the good soil of Jesus Christ. No tree can grow or bear fruit without sturdy and unwavering roots. Set aside time each day for prayer and reading the Bible. Discuss different ways that you can strengthen your relationships with God and others.

Week 10: Love

―――

"Teacher, which is the great commandment in the Law?" And he said to him, "You shall love the Lord your God with all your heart and with all your soul and with all your mind. This is the great and first commandment. And the second is like it: You shall love your neighbor as yourself. On these two commandments depend all the Law and the Prophets." MATTHEW 22:36–40

God loves us and we in return are to love Him. God created everything. He created the heavens and the earth, light and darkness, plants and animals, and you and me. God created all of the beauty of this world for us to enjoy. He created these things because He loves us. He wants us to be full of joy. All that He requires in return is that we accept his Son as our Savior. We are to love Him as He first loved us. We can never forget that our primary responsibility as Christians is to love God.

Jesus angered many of the religious leaders of the time with His message. Jesus taught that the love of God and loving others was more important than following a series of strict rules. Jesus promised salvation to all people through the grace of His Father and His sacrifice on the cross, not by doing good works or being a literary expert on the Old Testament. When we accept Jesus as our Savior, we are forever changed. We should continually further our understanding of God and Jesus' teachings. We have a responsibility to share the good news with everyone that God brings into our lives.

Jesus was being tested when He was asked what the most important commandment was according to the Law. Jesus replied that the great and first commandment is to love the Lord your God with every fiber of your being. Jesus passed every test that was given to Him during His life. His teachings were groundbreaking and threatened the leaders of the time, which eventually led to His death on the cross. Jesus knew that He had to be crucified for our salvation. It was His most important accomplishment. The death of Jesus released us from our sins. Jesus overcame death through His resurrection. He gave us the ability to have eternal life. God and His Son, Jesus, have done everything for us. How can we do anything but love someone who has given us so much?

HARVEST THE FRUIT: Focus on ways you can show your love for God. God has blessed each of us in so many ways. We are blessed to be born in a country with religious freedom to worship God. We can share the story of Jesus Christ with everyone we meet through our actions and our words. Show God you love Him by living a life worthy of the sacrifice Jesus made. Return God's love for you with unconditional love for Him and others.

Week 11: Joy

"Or what woman, having ten silver coins, if she loses one coin, does not light a lamp and sweep the house and seek diligently until she finds it? And when she has found it, she calls together her friends and neighbors, saying, 'Rejoice with me, for I have found the coin that I had lost.' Just so, I tell you, there is joy before the angels of God over one sinner who repents." LUKE 15:8–10

In the parable of the lost coin, Jesus used an analogy to compare a woman who loses a silver coin and searches until she finds it to a sinner who repents his sins and finds salvation. In both cases, there is great joy over finding that which was previously lost. Jesus often used parables to help people better comprehend His teachings. He spoke in terms His audience could easily understand so that nothing was misinterpreted. Jesus was careful to make sure that His teachings could be understood by everyone and would stand the test of time. His words are just as applicable today as they were when He spoke them.

Have you ever lost something and spent hours or even days trying to find it? It may be something of little significance or it could be of great importance. We are often willing to spend as much time as we need to find the lost item. We retrace our steps, think about when the last time we used or saw the item, and ask others if they have seen it. It is hard to stop looking for a lost item until it is found. Once it is found, the time and effort we spent searching are forgotten. We are happy we have found it. The same can be said when a person comes to know Jesus Christ on a personal level. There is joy before the angels of God.

We don't need to have perfect grammar, be a religious expert, or be a great public speaker to share the salvation of Jesus Christ with others. We simply need to have a profound love for God and for others. We have a duty to share the truth of Jesus Christ with the people that God brings into our lives. If we are willing to speak up and the other person is willing to listen, there will be much joy. Joy for the person saved. Joy for you knowing you helped lead someone to Christ. Joy in Heaven.

HARVEST THE FRUIT: Think about something very important to you that was lost but you later found. Think of what you went through or were willing to sacrifice until you found it. What did you feel like after you found what you were looking for? Did you have feelings of satisfaction, relief, happiness, and joy? Think about the joy in Heaven when someone asks Jesus Christ into their life. Is there someone you can share your faith with to help lead them to salvation? A person who is lost and repents is the most important thing that can be found.

Week 12: Peace

⁓

Rejoice in the Lord always; again I will say, Rejoice. Let your reasonableness be known to everyone. The Lord is at hand; do not be anxious about anything, but in everything by prayer and supplication with thanksgiving let your requests be made known to God. And the peace of God, which surpasses all understanding, will guard your hearts and your minds in Christ Jesus. Finally, brothers, whatever is true, whatever is honorable, whatever is just, whatever is pure, whatever is lovely, whatever is commendable, if there is any excellence, if there is anything worthy of praise, think about these things. What you have learned and received and heard and seen in me—practice these things, and the God of peace will be with you. PHILIPPIANS 4:4–9

Our lives continue to get more busy. We are occupied with work, taking care of the kids, doing chores around the house, and running errands. The list goes on and on. We rarely have time to quietly sit and reflect on our lives. When we do have a little extra time to relax, we are usually glued to the television, the computer, or our smartphone. Through social media and technology, we are connected to others in ways that were impossible only a few years ago. Technology is great and has made our lives better. Seeing status updates on your friends and family is a good way to see what is happening in their lives. Texting and social media should not be used to replace verbal communication with the people that you care about.

Busier lives lead to more anxiety and worries. Anxiety over our jobs, our finances, our health, and our loved ones. It is our human nature to worry about things. I don't believe that anyone will ever be able to say they have no worries in their life. However, we need to focus our energy on bringing our anxiety to the Lord through prayer. We should attempt to give all of our anxieties, our worries, and our stress to God. Ask Him to help us deal with the issues we are going through. We need to focus on the positive things in our lives instead of dwelling on the negative. Constantly worrying about things that are outside of our control has harmful impacts on our health and our relationships. Worrying has very little impact on what actually happens. Focus on the things you can control and give the rest to God.

We need to make time to quietly sit and reflect on the day's activities. Moments of peace where we can talk to God through prayer. Time set aside to thank God for the blessings He has provided in our lives. Time dedicated to give God our worries.

HARVEST THE FRUIT: Focus on being content and at peace in every aspect of your life. True peace can only be found through a personal relationship with Jesus Christ. Think about what causes anxiety and stress in your life. Consider all of the negative impacts that your worries have on you and your loved ones. It will not be easy, but instead of dwelling on the things that are causing your anxiety, pray about them. Give them to God and let His peace, which surpasses all understanding, fill your lives.

Week 13: Patience

Be patient, therefore, brothers, until the coming of the Lord. See how the farmer waits for the precious fruit of the earth, being patient about it, until it receives the early and the late rains. You also, be patient. Establish your hearts, for the coming of the Lord is at hand. Do not grumble against one another, brothers, so that you may not be judged; behold, the Judge is standing at the door. But above all, my brothers, do not swear, either by heaven or by earth or by any other oath, but let your "yes" be yes and your "no" be no, so that you may not fall under condemnation. JAMES 5:7–9, 12

It is hard to be patient. It is not in our nature. We have a tendency to seek instant gratification. We want things now, not later. Patience is a virtue, an essential quality that we should all attempt to attain. Being willing to wait for things and being content with what we currently have will help make our lives more enjoyable. It is especially important to teach the children in our lives the significance of being patient. Life will not always go exactly as we like, but having patience will allow us to weather the storms we face. Patience provides us with the ability to view the negative things in our lives as temporary. It encourages us to focus on the positive things that we have and those that are yet to come.

Be patient and trust in the Lord. God has a plan for each of us. He is always with us, and He knows what is best for us. We will experience hardships in life, but we should take comfort that everything happens according to God's will. We need to have confidence that no matter what difficulties we face in life, God is in control. If we are patient and keep a positive attitude, we can overcome any obstacles that we face. God has great things planned for each of us. Be patient, and place your faith in Him.

This week's Scripture reading also says to let your "yes" be yes and your "no" be no. We need to be truthful and honest with others. When we say we will do something, we should do it. Likewise, when we say we will not do something, we should make sure that we don't. Others should be able to listen to what we say and take it as a fact. Our words and our actions should be consistent with each other. If we live our lives in a manner that follows the teachings of Jesus, we should never need to swear that we will or won't do something. People will know that they can believe what we tell them.

HARVEST THE FRUIT: Focus on improving the patience you have with God. Put all of your trust in Him. Realize that He will never leave or forsake you. Discuss the areas that you need to work on to be more patient with God's plan for your life. Make a commitment to do what you say you will do. Be honest and truthful, so others can take you at your word and believe what you tell them.

Week 14: Kindness

And he opened his mouth and taught them, saying: "Blessed are the poor in spirit, for theirs is the kingdom of heaven. Blessed are those who mourn, for they shall be comforted. Blessed are the meek, for they shall inherit the earth. Blessed are those who hunger and thirst for righteousness, for they shall be satisfied. Blessed are the merciful, for they shall receive mercy. Blessed are the pure in heart, for they shall see God. Blessed are the peacemakers, for they shall be called sons of God. Blessed are those who are persecuted for righteousness' sake, for theirs is the kingdom of heaven. Blessed are you when others revile you and persecute you and utter all kinds of evil against you falsely on my account. Rejoice and be glad, for your reward is great in heaven, for so they persecuted the prophets who were before you." MATTHEW 5:2–12

This week's Scripture reading is commonly known as the Beatitudes. Jesus spoke these words as part of His Sermon on the Mount. He assures us that everyone is blessed, especially those experiencing hardships. The blessings that we have received through Jesus Christ will make any of the suffering that we experience in our lives worth it.

The Sermon on the Mount contains themes from the Old Testament but looks at them in a completely new manner. The sermon was a foundation of Jesus' ministry. It is one of the cornerstones of our Christian faith. Jesus' teachings were a radical transformation from the religious beliefs of that time. The Old Testament focuses heavily on specific rules that must be followed and the wrath of God toward those who sin. The Old Testament is still very important today, as it provides connections to the New Testament and makes God's Word complete. Jesus came to fulfill the true purpose of the Law in the Old Testament. The teachings of Jesus focused on love, mercy, and kindness. Jesus taught that salvation cannot be earned. Salvation is given to us through the grace of God and through Christ's sacrifice on the cross.

Life is difficult. We all experience pain and suffering. We can never lose sight of the fact that God loves us. We need to have faith that God is always with us. Through Jesus Christ, we have been given salvation. Never let go of the hope that we have received through Christ. We need to persevere. God promises that our suffering and pain are only temporary. When times get tough we can turn to Him for comfort. Make every effort to be merciful and kind to others, showing them the same compassion that we receive from our Father.

HARVEST THE FRUIT: Focus on the many blessings that God has given you. We will never have everything we want, but God has given us everything we need. Thank God for never leaving your side and for the salvation you have received through Jesus Christ. Encourage others who are suffering that it is only temporary. Reassure them that we have a great reward waiting for us in Heaven. Read the entire Sermon on the Mount in Matthew 5–7 to get a better understanding of Jesus' teachings.

Week 15: Goodness

As for you, always be sober-minded, endure suffering, do the work of an evangelist, fulfill your ministry. For I am already being poured out as a drink offering, and the time of my departure has come. I have fought the good fight, I have finished the race, I have kept the faith. Henceforth there is laid up for me the crown of righteousness, which the Lord, the righteous judge, will award to me on that Day, and not only to me but also to all who have loved his appearing. 2 TIMOTHY 4:5–8

When our time in this life is nearing its end, I hope that we can say the same thing Paul did in this week's Scripture reading. I have fought the good fight, I have finished the race, and I have kept the faith. We are called to put God first and the needs of others before our own. We should constantly search for ways to share the love we have for God with others. We should never stop praising God for everything He has done for us. Sharing the story of Jesus Christ is one of our most important responsibilities. The reward for living a life as God commands will far exceed our expectations.

It is difficult to share our faith with others. Talking about Jesus is hard, especially with people that we aren't particularly close to. The more we talk about our faith, the easier it becomes. We should always be careful that we don't sound condescending or act like we have all of the answers. We don't always have to use our words to share our faith story. Our actions are very powerful tools in showing others the love that we have for God and the love that we have for them. We should always treat others with respect and kindness. Be good to everyone, no matter how they treat you.

God wants us to have an interest in the lives of others. We all have our own issues to deal with, but we have a responsibility to be active in the lives of those around us. Ask others how they are doing. Take the time to let them know you care for them. If you know they are going through adversity, ask them if there is anything you can do to help. Be a better neighbor to everyone. Be willing to share your time and resources with others. Offer to help with yard work or chores around the house. There are many ways we can evangelize to others. God has blessed each of us with abilities that can help lead others to Him. Determine what skills you have been blessed with and use them to show goodness to others.

HARVEST THE FRUIT: Focus on living a meaningful life using the gifts and talents God has given you. Be certain you can say you have fought the good fight and finished the race. We are called to live a life with purpose, fulfilling the ministry God has put before us. Is there anything that you need to do in your life to ensure you are living up to this week's Scripture reading? There is no better time than now to make a change.

Week 16: Faithfulness

Not that I am speaking of being in need, for I have learned in whatever situation I am to be content. I know how to be brought low, and I know how to abound. In any and every circumstance, I have learned the secret of facing plenty and hunger, abundance and need. I can do all things through him who strengthens me.
PHILIPPIANS 4:11–13

An important step in having a joyful life is by learning to be content in every situation. No one has a perfect life and this world can be a difficult place. We all experience times of pain and suffering. We also experience times of great joy and jubilation. The Bible teaches us to be content no matter what we are going through. It is always easier to be content when everything is going well in our lives. We need to work on being content during the difficult times we face. It will be hard and it will take some effort, but we need to have faith that God is constantly working in our lives.

The only way to guarantee true peace and contentment is by completely submitting everything to God. By placing everything in God's hands, we put our trust in the only one who truly knows what we need. We can do all things through Christ, who gives us strength. Jesus is the Prince of Peace and the Wonderful Counselor. Through our faith, we can trust that God has a divine plan for us. God wants us to do great things. We should ask God to give us direction for our lives. Pray that we live our lives to the full potential we have been given. There is nothing beyond the power of our God. Anything can be accomplished when we rely completely on Him.

When we give our lives to Christ, we are immediately transformed. We are given the promise and gift of eternal life. This doesn't mean that our lives will be perfect or that we will never face struggles. It doesn't mean that our faith journey or purpose in life is complete. We are all works in progress. We must continually strive to become who God wants us to be. Some of you are blessed to know exactly what God's purpose is for you and are living your lives as God intended. Be thankful for the direction that you have received and be diligent in fulfilling God's plan for you. If you are searching for what God has planned for you, do not be discouraged. Continue to pray for direction, and trust that God is working in your life. Be patient and have faith. We are all exactly where God wants us to be at this particular moment.

HARVEST THE FRUIT: Focus on having complete and unwavering trust in God. Have faith that God has a plan for you and that He is always by your side. Strive to be content with the life you have been given. Discuss what you feel God's purpose is for you. Talk about the gifts that each of you have been blessed with. Pray that God gives you the strength and direction to live according to His plan.

Week 17: Gentleness

But even if you should suffer for righteousness' sake, you will
be blessed. Have no fear of them, nor be troubled, but in your
hearts honor Christ the Lord as holy, always being prepared
to make a defense to anyone who asks you for a reason for the
hope that is in you; yet do it with gentleness and respect, having
a good conscience, so that, when you are slandered, those who
revile your good behavior in Christ may be put to shame. For it
is better to suffer for doing good, if that should be God's will,
than for doing evil. 1 PETER 3:14–17

There are many reasons to be happy and hopeful in our lives. We
have a God who loves us unconditionally. We have a home in Heaven
once our time on earth has reached its end. People who have beliefs
different from us may attack and persecute us. We must be diligent in
keeping our faith and living the life God has called us to. We should
continually treat others with respect and kindness. We should show
love and gentleness to everyone no matter how badly they may treat
us. The Bible teaches us to have no fear and to not be troubled when
we are discriminated against because of our Christian beliefs. If
we suffer because of our faith in this life, we will be blessed in the
Kingdom of Heaven.

Hopefully you have never been persecuted because of your faith.
We live in a time and a country that allows for religious freedom.
We should never take these freedoms for granted. There are many
countries that persecute Christians. Christians can be subject to
harsh penalties or imprisoned for their faith. We are called to share

our Christian beliefs no matter what the outcome is. In Matthew 10:32–33, Jesus said,

> So everyone who acknowledges me before men, I also will acknowledge before my Father who is in heaven, but whoever denies me before men, I also will deny before my Father who is in heaven.

We are called to defend the hope that we have received through Jesus Christ to anyone who questions us. When sharing our faith, we need to be respectful of the other person. We should always remain humble and gentle. We should respond to their questions candidly but considerately. We have a responsibility to share our testimony and the love that we have for God with them. We should never be argumentative or let our pride get in the way of sharing the truth of Jesus Christ. Remember that God's message is more important than our own agenda. Always defend or share your faith with a gentle spirit.

HARVEST THE FRUIT: Focus on treating others with gentleness. Be humble and respectful at all times. Use your words and actions to influence others in a meaningful and lasting way. Remember that sharing our Christian beliefs with others is more important than our personal needs. Pray that God uses you for the benefit of His Kingdom. Ask Him to help you treat others with humility and grace.

Week 18: Self-Control

The end of all things is at hand; therefore be self-controlled and sober-minded for the sake of your prayers. Above all, keep loving one another earnestly, since love covers a multitude of sins. Show hospitality to one another without grumbling. As each has received a gift, use it to serve one another, as good stewards of God's varied grace: whoever speaks, as one who speaks oracles of God; whoever serves, as one who serves by the strength that God supplies—in order that in everything God may be glorified through Jesus Christ. To him belong glory and dominion forever and ever. Amen. 1 PETER 4:7–11

Only God knows when He will call us to our heavenly home. It could be today, next week, or years from now. We must be prepared for when that time comes. We need to live our lives disciplined in our Christian faith. We all have shortcomings. We have sinned and will continue to do so. We need to repent and ask God to forgive our sins. We should continually strive to live our lives to the best of our abilities. Our self-control is imperative to live how Jesus taught. Loving God, loving others, and loving ourselves. As this week's Scripture reading says, love covers a multitude of sins.

We all have God-given abilities. Special gifts that when combined no one else has. God gave us these traits to be champions for His cause. We should never use our abilities to take advantage of others or for our own selfish desires. God created us to love and serve others using the gifts that He has provided. The Holy Spirit gives each of us passions for certain things in life. Usually our passions are in direct correlation with our God-given abilities. When we follow our passions and use the gifts that God has provided, we can make this world a better place. Better for us knowing that we are living the life that God wants for us. Better for others when we make a positive and permanent impact in their lives.

We all have the option to stroll through life, never taking any risks. We can stay in the mundane job that provides financial security but we are not passionate about. It is often easier and more comfortable to just get by. If we do this, we will never reach our full potential. We need to be willing to step out of our comfort zones. It won't be easy and it will take self-control, but in doing so, we can live extraordinary lives. We can be an agent for change, making this world a better place for all of God's people.

HARVEST THE FRUIT: Focus on being prepared for when you are called to your heavenly home. Our time can come at any moment. Make sure that when you look back on your life, you don't regret how you chose to live. Discuss the God-given talents that each member of your family has. Discuss the passions that you have and how they relate to your gifts. Ask God to use you as an agent for His change. Pray for the strength and self-control to live an extraordinary life.

Week 19: Love

As the Father has loved me, so have I loved you. Abide in my love. If you keep my commandments, you will abide in my love, just as I have kept my Father's commandments and abide in his love. These things I have spoken to you, that my joy may be in you, and that your joy may be full. This is my commandment, that you love one another as I have loved you. Greater love has no one than this, that someone lay down his life for his friends. JOHN 15:9–13

Jesus commands us to love one another just as He loved us. This does not mean we only love people that let us have our way or have the same beliefs as us. It means we should love everybody. This is not always an easy thing to do. We all have our own desires and like to do things our own way. We have a tendency to think that we know what is the best for us and that others do not understand exactly what we need. When someone else's wants are contrary to ours and they go against our wishes, it can be hard to reach an agreement. God knows that we are all unique and different from each other. He created us that way. It would be an extremely boring world if everyone were the same. Our differences make life exciting and interesting. We will not always see things the same way or have the same ideas and opinions. We can still show love to everyone, including those who have different ideas, morals, and lifestyles.

Jesus shared his ministry with everyone. He did not limit his teachings to the popular, the wealthy, or the spiritual leaders. Everyone deserves and needs to hear of God's love and the story of Jesus Christ.

God did not create us to judge others and hold them accountable for their actions. That is God's responsibility. We are all held accountable for our actions and will have to answer to God when the time comes. God put us here to share the light and love of Jesus Christ with everyone we are able to. Showing love and respect to others is a great way to demonstrate the love God has for them. We all have the desire to feel loved by others. You have probably heard the saying "All we need is love." Although we do need things like food, water, shelter, and clothing, love is just as important.

HARVEST THE FRUIT: Focus on ways you can show love to others. Focus on the most important people in your life and show them unconditional love. Encourage a person who is going through a difficult time that you and God love them. Assure them you will help however you can. Jesus said we should love one another as He has loved us. Read the Ten Commandments that God gave to Moses in Exodus 20. Are there any changes that you need to make in your life to comply with God's commandments?

Week 20: Joy

Truly, truly, I say to you, you will weep and lament, but the world will rejoice. You will be sorrowful, but your sorrow will turn into joy. When a woman is giving birth, she has sorrow because her hour has come, but when she has delivered the baby, she no longer remembers the anguish, for joy that a human being has been born into the world. So also you have sorrow now, but I will see you again, and your hearts will rejoice, and no one will take your joy from you. In that day you will ask nothing of me. Truly, truly, I say to you, whatever you ask of the Father in my name, he will give it to you. Until now you have asked nothing in my name. Ask, and you will receive, that your joy may be full. JOHN 16:20–24

Jesus was preparing His followers for His upcoming death on the cross. He knew that the time was nearing for Him to complete His mission, providing salvation to all who follow Him. Jesus was preparing for the anguish that He would experience during His capture, torture, and crucifixion. Through all of this, He was still able to tell His followers that their sorrow would turn to joy. As the Son of God, His ultimate sacrifice was to die on the cross for our sins. He would overcome death three days later through His resurrection.

We need to take comfort and rejoice that our debt has been paid. Focus on the fact that our final destination has already been determined. We are all sinners and cannot earn salvation on our own. Christ's death and resurrection has provided us with the opportunity to have eternal life. With the acceptance of Jesus Christ as our Lord and Savior, we are guaranteed life after death. The loss of loved ones is one of the most difficult things that we experience in life. Through the pain and sorrow, we are able to find comfort from our God. We can rejoice knowing we will see our brothers and sisters in Christ again.

Our forever home in Heaven will be a perfect paradise with no suffering, sickness, or sorrow. We will never be able to fully comprehend what Heaven will be like until we experience it on our own. It will be more beautiful than anything we have ever seen. Our joy and happiness will be immeasurable and unending. We will never cease in the praising of our Creator. How can we not live our lives full of joy when we know where we are going?

HARVEST THE FRUIT: Tell your family and friends how much you appreciate them. Thank them for the joy they have brought to your life. If God has blessed you with children, discuss the feelings that you went through during your pregnancy. Talk to them about the joy you experienced on the day of their birth. If they are old enough, talk to them about the joy you felt when they were born again through Jesus Christ.

Week 21: Peace

Finally, all of you, have unity of mind, sympathy, brotherly love, a tender heart, and a humble mind. Do not repay evil for evil or reviling for reviling, but on the contrary, bless, for to this you were called, that you may obtain a blessing. For whoever desires to love life and see good days, let him keep his tongue from evil and his lips from speaking deceit; let him turn away from evil and do good; let him seek peace and pursue it. 1 PETER 3:8–11

We need to seek and pursue peace with everyone in our lives. The first place we should start is to be united with other fellow Christians. Too often as Christians, we are caught up in what type of church we attend. We focus on whether we are Catholic or Protestant, Methodist or Lutheran, Disciples of Christ or Presbyterian. We have different opinions on how our church services should be organized, the type of music we should sing to praise God, or how often we should partake in Holy Communion. Instead of focusing on our differences, we need to focus on the fact that we are Christians. We need to be unified in our Christian faith. We all need to work together to share the messages of faith, hope, love, and peace we have through our Savior, Jesus Christ.

Words are very powerful. They can build people up or tear them down. We need to have control over our tongues and watch what we say. We should never use our words in a manner that makes others feel like they are not important children of God. We should use our words to encourage others and give them a sense of worth. Likewise, the names of God and Jesus Christ are holy and are not to be used lightly. Unfortunately, much too often, their names are used in vain. Think carefully before you speak or act, so you don't say or do something that you will regret.

When someone is cruel to us or says something hurtful, our initial reaction is to retaliate and *fight fire with fire.* It is a part of our human nature to seek revenge on the people who hurt us. It is hard to show kindness to someone who mistreats us, but as Christians, we should strive to repay them with love. Take a few moments to collect your thoughts and show your oppressor love and kindness. Being kind and seeking peace will have a much bigger impact than retaliation. The words and actions we choose could help create a wonderful friendship or even help lead the other person to Christ.

HARVEST THE FRUIT: Focus on using your words to have a positive impact on the lives of others. Use your words to encourage and support others. Let your words and actions show others the love you have for them and for God. Do you take the Lord's name in vain? If so, work on training your mind and tongue to stop. If someone uses the Lord's name in vain, ask them to not use that language around you. It won't be easy, but it is our responsibility as Christians.

Week 22: Patience

Know this, my beloved brothers: let every person be quick to hear, slow to speak, slow to anger; for the anger of man does not produce the righteousness of God. Therefore put away all filthiness and rampant wickedness and receive with meekness the implanted word, which is able to save your souls. But be doers of the word, and not hearers only, deceiving yourselves.
JAMES 1:19–22

The Bible commands us to be quick to hear and slow to speak. Too often, it seems like we do the opposite. We have a tendency to believe that we have the best ideas. We want to be the first to share our opinions. We speak before we think about what we are saying. We spend too little time listening to others, or we interrupt them when we have a different thought. We quickly disregard what others say if it is contrary to our own views. Being a good listener and having the ability to see things from the perspective of others are important qualities to have. It is important to listen and think about what others say. As Christ commands, we need to put the needs of others first. Words can be hurtful. We should always take time to think before we speak.

We need to be patient with the people that God has placed in our lives. We all have diverse opinions and unique talents. These differences will undoubtedly lead to disagreements. Getting angry and personally attacking others is counterproductive. Having open communication and discussing all of the facts are important when making decisions. We should make sure that everyone involved has the opportunity to share their opinions. This will allow each person to gain a different perspective from their own. The best decisions are usually made when everyone has provided input and when they are made together.

We need to get off of the sidelines and into the game. It is important that we read the Bible, attend church regularly, and grow our personal relationship with God. However, we are called to an even higher standard as Christians. We need to take action and follow the examples of living a life of significance provided to us in the Bible. Jesus made his disciples fishers of men. They shared the love of God with everyone they encountered. They taught that life was about so much more than living for ourselves. We are called to live selflessly, sharing the hope and patience we have received from Jesus Christ with all humanity.

HARVEST THE FRUIT: Focus on being a better listener. Make a commitment to think before you speak. Discuss the areas that you need to work on from this week's Scripture reading. When disagreements arise, make sure that they are handled properly. Do not let anger control you or your actions. Dedicate yourself to being more than a hearer of the Word. Make your life extraordinary by submitting everything to God and by sharing your fruit with others.

Week 23: Kindness

A man who is kind benefits himself, but a cruel man hurts himself. The wicked earns deceptive wages, but one who sows righteousness gets a sure reward. Whoever is steadfast in righteousness will live, but he who pursues evil will die. Those of crooked heart are an abomination to the Lord, but those of blameless ways are his delight. Be assured, an evil person will not go unpunished, but the offspring of the righteous will be delivered. PROVERBS 11:17–21

Most of us have flown on a commercial airplane. You have probably heard the flight attendant's safety instruction that, in case of an emergency, you should put on your oxygen mask before assisting others. It makes sense to put yourself first in this situation. Once you have your mask on, you can then focus on helping the others around you. This is not how God calls us to live as Christians. We are to put the needs of others before our own. It is not easy to do, but caring more about the needs of others provides us with joy. Being kind to others benefits both the person receiving and the person showing the kindness. It is contagious. Think about a time when someone was kind to you. Did it inspire you to do something kind for them or for someone else? Take the lead in starting a repetitive cycle of kindness.

It can look like bad behavior gets rewarded in this life. It can also feel like honest behavior gets punished. It has been said that "God helps those who help themselves." It sometimes feels like this is the case in the world we live in. A classmate cheats on a test and gets a good grade. A coworker takes credit for work that they did not do and gets a promotion. There are countless other examples. Always remember that the outcomes of immoral behavior are not true rewards. They are only temporary. This week's Scripture reading assures us that sinful behavior yields deceiving results. It will not go unpunished.

Giving Jesus Christ complete control of our lives provides us with a sure and permanent reward. We should always focus on the everlasting gift that we will receive by putting Christ in the center of our lives. Being unconditionally kind and honest with others shows them that we are different. They will know that we are Christians. We should strive to always show love, mercy, and kindness to others as Jesus did.

HARVEST THE FRUIT: Focus on being kind to everyone. Be honest and righteous in all that you do. Discuss with your family someone that you have showed kindness to. How did your act of kindness impact both you and the other person? Never take the easy way out by cheating or being dishonest. Always remember that God provides a sure and true reward to those who live as He commands.

Week 24: Goodness

For in this hope we were saved. Now hope that is seen is not hope. For who hopes for what he sees? But if we hope for what we do not see, we wait for it with patience. Likewise the Spirit helps us in our weakness. For we do not know what to pray for as we ought, but the Spirit himself intercedes for us with groanings too deep for words. And he who searches hearts knows what is the mind of the Spirit, because the Spirit intercedes for the saints according to the will of God. And we know that for those who love God all things work together for good, for those who are called according to his purpose. ROMANS 8:24–28

The Holy Spirit is always by our side. He is there for us in the quiet times as well as the hectic. The Holy Spirit knows exactly what we need. His direction can be found when we deeply search our souls. If we calm our minds and explore our hearts, the Holy Spirit is the direct communication line from our heavenly Father. We all experience difficult times in our lives, but we need to have faith that God's love is never-ending. Continue to love and trust God. Everything will work out according to His plan. We can rest assured that He has good things planned for those who love Him.

Think about all of the ways God has blessed you and your loved ones. I have truly been blessed in this life with a great family. Both of my parents are loving Christians and still have an active role in my life. They have always been supportive of me as a child and as an adult. I am blessed with two wonderful siblings who are two of my best friends. They have wonderful spouses and children. God has also blessed me with a loving wife, Rachel. She is one of the kindest and sweetest people that I have ever met. I thank God every day for the wonderful family He has given me. We all have been blessed by God in many ways. We need to stay focused on our blessings instead of dwelling on the disappointing things in our lives.

No one has a perfect life. We all experience troubled times. We go through difficulties and hardships. Everyone handles suffering differently. The one thing that is the same for everyone is that God is with us in every situation we endure. We must constantly believe that everything will work out for the best. Completely trust in God. We need to be patient and have faith in God. When people we know are going through difficult times, we should provide them support in whatever way we can. Make sure that they know we are never alone. God's goodness is always present.

HARVEST THE FRUIT: Focus on being patient and wait for God to work His plan for your life. Calm your minds and search your hearts for direction from the Holy Spirit. Ask God to make you His instrument. Think about the various ways God has shown you His goodness. Be thankful for God's goodness, and pray that He continues to bless your loved ones. Trust that God has great things planned for you.

Week 25: Faithfulness

And Jesus rebuked the demon, and it came out of him, and the boy was healed instantly. Then the disciples came to Jesus privately and said, "Why could we not cast it out?" He said to them, **"Because of your little faith. For truly, I say to you, if you have faith like a grain of mustard seed, you will say to this mountain, 'Move from here to there,' and it will move, and nothing will be impossible for you."** MATTHEW 17:18–20

It is difficult to believe in things that we cannot see or don't fully comprehend. We want concrete, indisputable evidence that we can see or touch. With our limited human understanding, we want to see proof before we believe. Even the disciples who saw Jesus perform numerous miracles had doubts. The disciples saw Jesus turn water into wine, heal the lame and the blind, and even raise the dead. They still had doubts that Jesus overcame His death on the cross until they could see for themselves. Through the grace of God, we only need to have a little faith. Jesus said that with faith as small as a mustard seed, nothing is impossible.

We can learn a lot from the children in our lives. Children are not skeptical and pessimistic like adults are. They are trusting, always seeing the best in others. They are willing to believe in the impossible and have wonderful imaginations. If we could be more like children in these ways, the world would be a much better place. Jesus loves children. He said to not hinder the children from coming to Him. We have a responsibility to make sure that the children in our lives know they are special and loved. We need to continually encourage them to follow their hearts and to trust that God is working in their lives. We also need to make sure that we never take advantage of a child's trust.

We will never have enough faith to perform miracles on our own. What we can do is have faith that God performs miracles every day. God makes the impossible possible. He leads people to medical discoveries that improve and save lives. He heals people who were not expected to live. Through prayer, nothing is beyond the power of God. By placing our complete trust in God, we know that everything will work out according to His plan. We can never forget that a little bit of faith goes a long way.

HARVEST THE FRUIT: Focus on having faith like that of a child. Continually work on increasing your faith in God. Remember that nothing is impossible through Him. Tell the children in your life how much you appreciate their optimism and trusting nature. Make sure that they know they are unique and treasured children of God. We should never stop showing and telling the children in our lives that they are loved.

Week 26: Gentleness

Remind them to be submissive to rulers and authorities, to
be obedient, to be ready for every good work, to speak evil of
no one, to avoid quarreling, to be gentle, and to show perfect
courtesy toward all people. For we ourselves were once foolish,
disobedient, led astray, slaves to various passions and pleasures,
passing our days in malice and envy, hated by others and hating
one another. But when the goodness and loving kindness of God
our Savior appeared, he saved us, not because of works done
by us in righteousness, but according to his own mercy, by the
washing of regeneration and renewal of the Holy Spirit, whom he
poured out on us richly through Jesus Christ our Savior, so that
being justified by his grace we might become heirs according to
the hope of eternal life. TITUS 3:1–7

We are called to be obedient to those God places in positions of
authority. We can never forget that God is in control of everything.
He has an active role in determining the authority figures in our
lives. Whether it is our parents, our bosses, our teachers, our religious
leaders, or our world leaders, we are to be respectful and subservient.
We should follow their lead and listen to their instructions. We
should always be courteous. As Jesus proclaimed, it is our duty as
Christians to serve others and not to be served.

When leaders abuse their power, we have a responsibility to
be a voice for change. We should candidly and civilly discuss the
injustices that are taking place. We should never be afraid to speak
up when someone is misusing their God-given authority. It is our

duty as Christians to continually strive to make this world a better place for all humanity. Our efforts should be done openly by using whatever platform God grants us. We need to be courageous and willing to discuss our concerns directly with the wrongdoers. We should always be polite and respectful when talking with others about the issues that we are trying to correct.

Jesus provided us with perfect examples of how to deal with people who abuse their power. Many of the leaders of Jesus' time were abusing their authority. Jesus was tested by them numerous times, hoping that He would fail in His mission. He never did. Jesus was an eloquent speaker and was willing to speak up when He saw injustices. He was gentle and candid. According to God's plan, Jesus ultimately gave His life because the leaders of the time were threatened by His teachings. Through His grace and our faith, we have been given eternal life.

HARVEST THE FRUIT: Focus on being submissive to those in positions of authority. Remember that everything happens according to God's plan. We all have a platform that we can use to be a voice for change. When people in authority abuse their power, we have a duty to speak up about the injustices. Do you know of someone who is abusing their authority? Be willing to openly and politely discuss your concerns. Take action to make this world a better place.

Week 27: Self-Control

To the weak I became weak, that I might win the weak. I have become all things to all people, that by all means I might save some. I do it all for the sake of the gospel, that I may share with them in its blessings. Do you not know that in a race all the runners run, but only one receives the prize? So run that you may obtain it. Every athlete exercises self-control in all things. They do it to receive a perishable wreath, but we an imperishable. So I do not run aimlessly; I do not box as one beating the air. But I discipline my body and keep it under control, lest after preaching to others I myself should be disqualified. 1 CORINTHIANS 9:22–27

God provides us with a human form that we need to take care of. Living a healthy life requires self-control and discipline. We should exercise regularly and be mindful of the things that we put into our bodies. We should eat healthier and only drink alcohol in moderation if we are of legal age. We should be faithful to our spouse. Our bodies are temples that should be used to glorify God. When we take care of our bodies, we please our Creator. We are treating the vessel that God created with care and respect.

Some of the health issues that we face in our lives are beyond our control. There are many diseases that affect healthy people who have taken great care of themselves. With all of the things that are outside of our control, it is important that we take the steps to prevent health issues that are within our control. Obesity can lead to numerous health issues, including heart disease, increased risk of having a stroke, and diabetes. Smoking is a leading cause of cancer and numerous lung diseases. These are just a few examples of harmful behaviors that we have control over. There are numerous others. If you are harming your health with actions that are within your control, take steps to correct them. Seeking help for addiction or other issues that we face in life is a sign of strength, not of weakness.

It is important to have self-control in every aspect of our lives. It allows others to see that we are answering to a higher power. Through living disciplined lives, others see that we are living for something greater than ourselves. When we maintain a healthy lifestyle, it allows us to fully reach the potential God has given us. We are only given one life and one body; make the most of them.

HARVEST THE FRUIT: Focus on having the discipline to live a healthy lifestyle. Exercising with family members and friends is a great way to strengthen your relationships and your bodies. Take steps to correct the behaviors and actions in your life that have negative results. We only have one shot at life on earth. Make the most of your life by having self-control. Have the strength to ask for help if you are having trouble overcoming the issues that have negative impacts on you or your loved ones.

Week 28: Love

Do not love the world or the things in the world. If anyone loves the world, the love of the Father is not in him. For all that is in the world—the desires of the flesh and the desires of the eyes and pride in possessions—is not from the Father but is from the world. And the world is passing away along with its desires, but whoever does the will of God abides forever. 1 JOHN 2:15–17

We should all enjoy life and live our lives to the fullest, but we should never love the world or the things of the world. We are only here for a short amount of time. We have a responsibility to make the most out of the time we are given to share the love of God with everyone we meet. The world and the things in it are only temporary. Nothing in this life is truly ours; everything is God's. Money, wealth, cars, houses, clothes, toys, and all of "our" worldly possessions will not last. Only God is timeless. He is the Alpha and the Omega, who is and who was and who is to come.

There is a big difference between something that we need and something that we want. Many people often confuse the two. A need is something that we require in order to survive, such as oxygen, food, water, shelter, and clothing. God is our biggest need. A want is something that we often think that we need but is only something that we desire. We can live without it. The newest smartphone, the large, flat-screen television, the latest designer fashions, or multiple homes are examples of worldly things that we want but don't truly need. Make sure that you and your family know the difference between what you need and what you want.

Many people go through life trying to accumulate as many worldly things as they can. They believe the more possessions they have, the happier they will be or the more successful they will appear. We are a society of consumers and are constantly looking to own the next best thing. The next best thing is the same as it has always been. It is the same as it will always be. God's love for us, loving God and others, and living lives that follow the teachings of Jesus Christ is and will always be the way to experience true joy and contentment. Giving our lives to Christ is also the only way to experience everlasting life.

HARVEST THE FRUIT: Focus on the permanent heavenly treasures that you have received. Do you have an issue with accumulating and loving the things of this world? Remember that the possessions you accumulate are only temporary and will not provide true happiness. When we love our possessions we will never be satisfied and we will always want more. True joy and contentment can only be known by having a personal relationship with our heavenly Father, the One who created us and knows exactly what we need.

Week 29: Joy

We ask you, brothers, to respect those who labor among you and are over you in the Lord and admonish you, and to esteem them very highly in love because of their work. Be at peace among yourselves. And we urge you, brothers, admonish the idle, encourage the fainthearted, help the weak, be patient with them all. See that no one repays anyone evil for evil, but always seek to do good to one another and to everyone. Rejoice always, pray without ceasing, give thanks in all circumstances; for this is the will of God in Christ Jesus for you. 1 THESSALONIANS 5:12–18

The world needs leaders. People with the vision to make lives better, to solve problems or provide guidance and instruction. We also need leaders in the Christian faith and in our churches. People who are willing to offer their time, talents, and resources to further the Kingdom of God. To provide answers and insights on what it truly means to be a Christian. Without the leaders of the early Christian church like Paul, who wrote this book and nearly half of the books in the New Testament, Christianity would probably be very different today. Leaders make a lasting impact on our lives and on the world.

We have a responsibility to use the talents and gifts God has given us to help others. We may not all be leaders, but we all have gifts that can be used to lead others to Christ. We may have a compassionate heart, a generous spirit, a way with words, or be a great listener. We need to use our talents to support and encourage others. When necessary, we should caution others when they are going down a path that contradicts our Christian faith. We should always strive to treat others in the same way that we like to be treated.

In all that we do, we should focus on having a good attitude and a thankful spirit. Life can be hard, but we always have something to celebrate. We have been given so much and need to be joyful. We need to spend time each day in prayer. Focus on living our lives for God and for others instead of living for ourselves. We can then experience the true joy of having a life with meaning.

HARVEST THE FRUIT: Tell the Christian leaders in your church and your community how thankful you are for them. Encourage them to keep fighting the good fight and sharing the love of Christ with others. Is there someone at work, school, or in your community that needs support or is going through a hard time? Make an effort to help them with an encouraging word, being a friend when they need one, or praying with and for them. Pray diligently for your family, your friends, church members, world leaders, the poor, and the lost. Be joyful for everything God has provided.

Week 30: Peace

Therefore, since we have been justified by faith, we have peace with God through our Lord Jesus Christ. Through him we have also obtained access by faith into this grace in which we stand, and we rejoice in hope of the glory of God. More than that, we rejoice in our sufferings, knowing that suffering produces endurance, and endurance produces character, and character produces hope, and hope does not put us to shame, because God's love has been poured into our hearts through the Holy Spirit who has been given to us. ROMANS 5:1–5

Have you or someone you know run in a long race? You don't just show up the day of the event and run when the race begins. You start training months in advance to build up your endurance, so you can perform to the best of your abilities on race day. Training and practice are nearly as important as the actual competition. No one can be successful in sports or competition by just showing up when it is time to compete. We have to put in the extra effort to reach our full potential. We must go through the process of getting our bodies and minds prepared. We need to be ready for whatever comes our way. The struggles that we endure during our training make the final results much more rewarding.

The same can be said of the suffering we experience in our lives. The Scripture reading says we should rejoice in our suffering as suffering produces endurance, endurance produces character, and character produces hope. The struggles we face in life shape and mold us into the people God wants us to be. God has a plan for each of us. He will never give us more than we can handle. It may feel like you have reached a breaking point, but God is always by your side. When you feel like all is lost and you can't go any further, turn to God and the people He puts in your life for support.

Our lives are more like a marathon than a sprint. There will be ups and downs along the way. We will experience moments of incredible happiness and excruciating sadness. No matter what life has in store for us, we need to find peace. Perfect peace that comes from the love of God and our faith in Jesus Christ. Peace knowing we are able to overcome anything when we rely completely on God.

HARVEST THE FRUIT: Think about one of your greatest and proudest accomplishments. Was the journey to reaching your goal always easy with no setbacks? How much greater was the satisfaction you experienced because of the difficulties you overcame? Remember to keep a positive outlook in every situation and be at peace with your decisions after prayerfully considering them. We don't know what God has planned for us, but we can be sure that He is our biggest fan.

Week 31: Patience

Blessed be the God and Father of our Lord Jesus Christ, the Father of mercies and God of all comfort, who comforts us in all our affliction, so that we may be able to comfort those who are in any affliction, with the comfort with which we ourselves are comforted by God. For as we share abundantly in Christ's sufferings, so through Christ we share abundantly in comfort too. If we are afflicted, it is for your comfort and salvation; and if we are comforted, it is for your comfort, which you experience when you patiently endure the same sufferings that we suffer. 2 CORINTHIANS 1:3–6

When we give our lives to Jesus Christ, we become one in the body of Christ. We can find reassurance in the fact that we have a God who is compassionate and loves us. Be patient and trust that the Lord will provide us with comfort in our times of need. Just as God comforts us during our afflictions, we are called to do the same for others. It is encouraging to know that we have a God who cares for us. Always remember that there are fellow Christians praying for us when we are going through difficulties in life.

Diligently pray for others who are suffering. Ask God to comfort them. Ask your family and friends to pray for them as well. Be sympathetic to the pain others are experiencing. Let others know that you are there for them in their times of need. Be willing to give them an uplifting and encouraging word. Take the time to sit down with them. Let them talk about what they are going through. Sometimes what people need the most is to have someone be there for them by listening and being a shoulder to cry on. Most importantly, make sure that they know they are a child of God and that He loves them.

Jesus Christ provided us with the standard on which we should model our lives. He showed compassion to everyone. He gave His life for us. He gave us hope for a future free from the bonds of sin. The comfort that He provides us is beyond our human capacity and more than we deserve. We have a responsibility to live our lives in a manner that is worthy of the sacrifice Jesus made for us. It is a lofty goal and one that we will never be able to fully reach, but we should continually strive to attain it.

HARVEST THE FRUIT: Focus on how you can provide comfort to someone who is in need. Let them know you are praying for them and you are willing to help them in whatever way you can. Reassure them that God loves them and that He is always with us. Make sure they know you are hurting for them. Encourage them to patiently wait for God's comfort. Reassure them that He will provide peace.

Week 32: Kindness

Give to everyone who begs from you, and from one who takes away your goods do not demand them back. And as you wish that others would do to you, do so to them. If you love those who love you, what benefit is that to you? For even sinners love those who love them. But love your enemies, and do good, and lend, expecting nothing in return, and your reward will be great, and you will be sons of the Most High, for he is kind to the ungrateful and the evil. Be merciful, even as your Father is merciful. LUKE 6:30–32, 35–36

How many times have you been approached by someone that has asked you for money? What was your response? Our initial response is often to speculate about what the person will use the money for. We are concerned they might waste the money on alcohol, illegal drugs, cigarettes, or lottery tickets. We worry that we could be causing them more harm than good. They could use the money to satisfy an addiction that they have. We fear they could rob us when we take out our wallets. These are all valid concerns, but we are called to be compassionate. We should be careful so that we don't endanger ourselves or our families when helping people that we don't know, but we should always try to help when we can.

Jesus calls us to give to everyone who begs from us and to treat others the way that we want to be treated. He also commands us to love our enemies. It is not always easy to live in a manner consistent with Christ's teachings. We can all do a better job of showing kindness and compassion to others, particularly to people who have mistreated us. We should constantly strive to live up to the standards that Jesus has set for us. We should continually attempt to show kindness and mercy to others, especially to those who are in need. Our reward will greatly exceed our efforts.

The next time someone asks you for money, take a moment to talk to them if you feel safe. Ask them if you can take them to a restaurant or buy them a meal. Have a conversation and get to know them. Talk to them about Jesus and what He has meant in your life. Tell them that God loves them and that they are a special child of God. We never know who God will bring into our lives. Taking the time to help a person in need is often a blessing for us as well.

HARVEST THE FRUIT: Make a commitment to give your time and resources to anyone who asks of you. Realize that we are all children of God. Show everyone the kindness and love that you would like to receive if you were in their situation. Discuss with your family a time when you helped someone in need or when you were in need and someone helped you. Talk about the blessings you have received through random acts of kindness.

Week 33: Goodness

I will extol you, my God and King, and bless your name forever and ever. Every day I will bless you and praise your name forever and ever. Great is the Lord, and greatly to be praised, and his greatness is unsearchable. One generation shall commend your works to another, and shall declare your mighty acts. On the glorious splendor of your majesty, and on your wondrous works, I will meditate. They shall speak of the might of your awesome deeds, and I will declare your greatness. They shall pour forth the fame of your abundant goodness and shall sing aloud of your righteousness. The Lord is gracious and merciful, slow to anger and abounding in steadfast love. The Lord is good to all, and his mercy is over all that he has made. PSALM 145:1–9

Our God is an awesome God! His love and goodness toward us are never-ending. He deserves all of our praise and gratitude. We should relentlessly worship Him, declaring His mighty splendor. We have a responsibility to share His marvelous works with everyone we meet. His name is holy. His power is infinite. God's greatness and mercy are beyond all human understanding. He alone is worthy of being called our Lord.

"God is good all the time, and all the time God is good." Many of you have heard this saying before. This quote was used several times in the wonderful movie *God's Not Dead.* The movie follows the lives of numerous people with a variety of different backgrounds and beliefs. The main storyline focuses on a freshman college student and his atheist professor. On the first day of class, the professor asks all of his students to write, "God is dead," on a sheet of paper, sign their name, and turn it in. Every student in the class follows his instructions except for one. A Christian student stands up for his faith. He refuses to follow the professor's demands. The student is forced to provide evidence and convince his fellow students that God is not dead. He faces the possibility of ruining his academic career along with his desire to become an attorney. His willingness to stand up for his faith has a permanent impact on his classmates and his professor.

We all have a platform on which we can share our faith with others. It is important to use whatever platform we have been given to further God's Kingdom. It is not always easy, but it is one of our main responsibilities as Christians. We should never be embarrassed or ashamed to share our faith with others. Jesus said if we are ashamed of Him or His Word, He will be ashamed of us.

HARVEST THE FRUIT: Focus on the greatness of our God. He is the Creator of everything. Watch the movie *God's Not Dead* and experience the wonderful ways God works in our lives. Discuss the opportunities that you have to use your platform to share your faith with the people that God brings into your life. Dedicate your life to be a shining example of the goodness that God shows to all of us.

Week 34: Faithfulness

And a great windstorm arose, and the waves were breaking into the boat, so that the boat was already filling. But he was in the stern, asleep on the cushion. And they woke him and said to him, "Teacher, do you not care that we are perishing?" And he awoke and rebuked the wind and said to the sea, "Peace! Be still!" And the wind ceased, and there was a great calm. He said to them, "Why are you so afraid? Have you still no faith?" And they were filled with great fear and said to one another, "Who then is this, that even the wind and the sea obey him?" MARK 4:37–41

Jesus had just finished a day of preaching to the crowds in Galilee. During the evening, He and His disciples got on a boat to go to the other side of the Sea of Galilee. While they were crossing the sea, a large storm arose that nearly capsized them. It was dark and the boat was being tossed around violently. The disciples became very afraid, fearing for their lives. Through all of the chaos, Jesus remained asleep. Jesus' faith was so strong that, even during the violent storm, He did not worry. He completely trusted His Father. The disciples frantically woke up Jesus and asked Him why He didn't care that they were about to perish. When Jesus awoke, He commanded the storm to stop. It immediately became still.

Jesus had already performed numerous miracles prior to calming the storm. He had cast out demons, healed a paralytic, and healed the sick. The disciples were able to see many of Jesus' miracles in person, but they still had their doubts. When the storm arose and their lives were in danger, their faith was tested. The disciples quickly forgot that they were with the Son of God. There was nothing to fear.

We all face storms in our lives. We lose loved ones, have health issues, face financial difficulties, or feel like we are alone. It is during these storms that our faith is tested. It is also during these times that our faith is the most important. We can never lose sight of the fact that God is always with us. By putting our complete trust in God, we can overcome any obstacles in life. We can find comfort that God knows exactly what we are going through. Our faith can help us overcome even the darkest times of our lives. Peace! Be still!

HARVEST THE FRUIT: Focus on strengthening your faith during the difficult times of your life. Trust that God is always working in your life. We all face storms and have our faith tested. Remember to keep your faith no matter what obstacles you face. Discuss some of the difficulties you have previously faced and how God helped you overcome them. Encourage others who are hurting that God is always with them.

Week 35: Gentleness

At that time Jesus declared, "I thank you, Father, Lord of heaven and earth, that you have hidden these things from the wise and understanding and revealed them to little children; yes, Father, for such was your gracious will. All things have been handed over to me by my Father, and no one knows the Son except the Father, and no one knows the Father except the Son and anyone to whom the Son chooses to reveal him. Come to me, all who labor and are heavy laden, and I will give you rest. Take my yoke upon you, and learn from me, for I am gentle and lowly in heart, and you will find rest for your souls. For my yoke is easy, and my burden is light." MATTHEW 11:25–30

We will never completely understand our wonderful and sovereign God. We could devote our entire lifetime to studying the Bible but only scratch the surface of comprehending our awesome God. God does not expect us to know everything about Him, His creation, or Heaven. God wants to keep some of His glorious mysteries beyond our human knowledge. We do not need to be biblical or religious experts to receive eternal life. We only need to believe in Jesus Christ with faith like that of a child.

We can only receive salvation through the acceptance of Jesus Christ as our Lord and Savior. As the Father's Son, Jesus was the only human who truly knew the Father. The Father gave everything to His Son. He was revealed to us when Jesus came to be the sacrifice for our sins. No one can know the Father without having a personal relationship with Jesus Christ. When Jesus died, the Holy Spirit was sent to be our guide. The Holy Spirit is always with us. The Holy Spirit works in us and through us doing God's will. Father, Son, and Holy Spirit. Through the blessed Trinity, God in three persons, we are able to have a personal relationship with our majestic God.

We have a gentle and caring God. He calls all who labor and are burdened to Him. When we work for and with God, we will never labor in vain. We find comfort by giving our troubles to Him. He is there to help us get through anything and everything that we face in life. God's compassionate hands hold us in the good times and the bad. His love and gentleness are beyond compare.

HARVEST THE FRUIT: Focus on giving your worries and burdens to our gentle and caring God. Accept God's love and direction in your life. He will give rest to your soul. Realize that we will never comprehend all of God's marvelous mysteries. Be willing to accept all of God's mercies without fully understanding His wonders. Be thankful that God sent His son to offer us the promise of everlasting life.

Week 36: Self-Control

Children, obey your parents in the Lord, for this is right. "Honor your father and mother" (this is the first commandment with a promise), "that it may go well with you and that you may live long in the land." Fathers, do not provoke your children to anger, but bring them up in the discipline and instruction of the Lord.
EPHESIANS 6:1–4

Every relationship is a two-way street. There must be compromise for a relationship to be successful and thrive. Open communication with a willingness by both parties to work through any issues that arise are necessities. The strongest relationships are built on a foundation of mutual respect and trust. These things are also applicable in the relationships between parents and their children. Clearly, parents have the majority of the control in the relationship, but children deserve to have some input as well.

God commands children to honor their father and mother. Children should always respect and obey their parents. Parents need to teach their children that this is God's commandment. When children honor their parents through their words and actions, they are honoring God. It is important for children to understand that when they are disciplined, it is done out of love. We should always assure the children in our lives that we want the best for them.

Parents need to raise their children under the discipline and instruction of the Lord. Time should be dedicated for the entire family to grow closer to God and to each other. Families should make time to pray together. Parents have an important spiritual responsibility to their children. Parents must diligently plant the seeds of faith in their children. You can't force your child to accept Jesus Christ as their Savior. You can only plant the seed and pray continually that your child asks Christ to lead their lives.

Relationships are hard work and require both parties to be actively engaged. God created us to be in a personal relationship with Him and with the people He places in our lives. Life is much better when we share it with others. When disagreements arise, the first question that both parties should ask is this: "What would God have me do in this situation?" After answering that question and discussing it with each other, it is much more likely that a compromise will be reached. A result that is pleasing to God.

HARVEST THE FRUIT: Focus on honoring your father and mother. Treat your parents with respect and admiration. Make sure to let your parents know how much you love and appreciate them. Continually show and tell the children in your life that you love them. You can never say, "I love you," too many times. Let your children know that when you discipline them, it is because you want the best for them.

Week 37: Love

———

If I speak in the tongues of men and of angels, but have not love, I am a noisy gong or a clanging cymbal. And if I have prophetic powers, and understand all mysteries and all knowledge, and if I have all faith, so as to remove mountains, but have not love, I am nothing. If I give away all I have, and if I deliver up my body to be burned, but have not love, I gain nothing. Love is patient and kind; love does not envy or boast; it is not arrogant or rude. It does not insist on its own way; it is not irritable or resentful; it does not rejoice at wrongdoing, but rejoices with the truth. Love bears all things, believes all things, hopes all things, endures all things. So now faith, hope, and love abide, these three; but the greatest of these is love. 1 CORINTHIANS 13:1–7, 13

These verses are familiar to most of you. You have probably attended a wedding that included at least part of this chapter in the Scripture reading. Love is the most important aspect of our lives. It is more important than money, success, power, knowledge, and self-sacrifice. Love is all-powerful and never-ending. Without love, our lives do not have meaning. Giving our complete love to God and showing our love to others are the most important things that we can do in our lives.

The chapter goes on to discuss what love is and what love isn't. It serves as a guideline of what true love really means. It is not always easy to like everyone, but we should always love them. Everyone has different characteristics and ideas that don't always coincide with our own. Jealousy, anger, and resentment are often our first responses when it feels like we aren't being treated fairly or when someone else has received something that we feel we deserve. But if we truly love others, as we are told to in the Bible, we should be happy for others when they are blessed in life.

No matter how much we have, there will always be someone who has more. We must always remember that the things of this world are only temporary. Life is not a competition to see who can make the most money or have the most possessions. We should constantly strive to love God, love others, and love ourselves. Use the love that God has for us as the example of how we love others.

HARVEST THE FRUIT: Focus on the love you have for God and for others. How does your love measure up to the love God has for you? Our love will never compare to the love we receive from God, but we should always use His love as the standard we strive for. If you are married, watch your wedding video or look at your wedding album with your spouse and your family. Have you kept the promises that you made to God and each other? If anything is lacking, make an effort to correct it now. Continually work on your marriage to make it an example of love for others to follow.

Week 38: Joy

I will instruct you and teach you in the way you should go; I will counsel you with my eye upon you. Be not like a horse or a mule, without understanding, which must be curbed with bit and bridle, or it will not stay near you. Many are the sorrows of the wicked, but steadfast love surrounds the one who trusts in the Lord. Be glad in the Lord, and rejoice, O righteous, and shout for joy, all you upright in heart! PSALM 32:8–11

Everlasting love surrounds those who place their trust in God! The Bible is the instruction manual for living a Christian life. It is God's Word and one of the ways He communicates to us. The Bible is one of the most important tools that we have at our disposal when it comes to living a life worthy of the sacrifice Jesus Christ made for us. We need to be knowledgeable and value the Word of God. We all have busy lives, but we need to set aside time to gain a better understanding of the Bible. It is an important step in growing our faith.

It is also important that we have fellowship with other Christians. Finding a good church family and attending church regularly are essential. Spending time with and worshiping our God with other Christians gives us a purpose. It provides us with a sense of belonging. It allows us to share how God is working in our lives. It shows us how God is working in the lives of others. Whenever possible, attend church with your family. It is a great way for a family to spend time with each other and grow closer together. It also shows your children that being a part of a church family is imperative.

We all like to consider ourselves experts in something. We may be experts at our jobs, our hobbies, our favorite games, or our favorite television shows. We know nearly everything there is to know about it. We dedicate our time and efforts to gain a better understanding of the subject. We spend hours perfecting our knowledge or skills. It is healthy to have a passion for something. It helps give our lives meaning. We should never lose sight of God and always make sure that becoming an expert in living a Christian life is our first priority. We can then experience a life full of joy.

HARVEST THE FRUIT: Make a commitment to gain a deeper understanding of God. Praise the Lord in every situation. Dedicate yourself and your family to spending more time with God through the reading of the Bible, praying with and for each other, and attending church. The Bible is God's Word and contains the guidelines for living a life that is pleasing to Him. We have so many reasons to be joyful, the most important being the promise of eternal life through our Savior, Jesus Christ. Focus on the things that bring joy to your life.

Week 39: Peace

For the moment all discipline seems painful rather than pleasant, but later it yields the peaceful fruit of righteousness to those who have been trained by it. Therefore lift your drooping hands and strengthen your weak knees, and make straight paths for your feet, so that what is lame may not be put out of joint but rather be healed. Strive for peace with everyone, and for the holiness without which no one will see the Lord. HEBREWS 12:11–14

No one likes to be disciplined. Who enjoys getting a speeding ticket, being reprimanded at school or work, or being grounded? It is usually unpleasant for both the person giving and the person receiving the discipline. It is uncomfortable to point out other people's mistakes and even more so to have others point out our mistakes. Rules are an important part of life. They hold people accountable for their actions. They provide guidance to correct inappropriate behavior. Without a system of rules and consequences for breaking those rules, society would quickly turn to chaos. However, we need to make sure that the rules do not infringe on anyone's God-given rights and that the punishment for breaking the rules is appropriate. Thankfully, we are blessed to live in a country where we have numerous rights, including the freedom to worship God how we please.

The Scripture reading for this week discusses the long-term impacts of discipline. Although discipline is painful at first, its end result is righteousness. Every person is unique and responds differently to various forms of discipline. You know what discipline works the best for your children. Whether that is a timeout, removing privileges or toys, or a reasonable spanking on the behind. Whatever it may be, we need to always remember that there is a fine line between some forms of discipline and abuse. Be careful that the line is never crossed. The punishment should never be more severe than what it takes to correct the inappropriate behavior. Proper discipline should only be used to correct unsuitable behavior. It should never be done in anger or to belittle another person. It should always be done out of love. Never forget to praise children when they are good. Positive reinforcement is one of the best ways to prevent the behaviors that need to be punished.

As a child, I was spanked when I misbehaved. I always knew my parents were disciplining me out of love and not out of anger. It was probably hurting them more than it hurt me. I am thankful that my parents raised my siblings and me in a strong Christian home. Their parenting taught us right from wrong. They helped shape us into the adults we are now.

HARVEST THE FRUIT: Talk to your family about discipline and being held accountable for our actions. Discuss the rules of your home. Make sure that it is clear what the consequences will be when the rules are broken. Reassure the children in your life that when they are disciplined it is out of love. We discipline the people we love because it teaches them right from wrong. It helps us grow. Encourage children to become the people God wants them to be.

Week 40: Patience

I therefore, a prisoner for the Lord, urge you to walk in a manner worthy of the calling to which you have been called, with all humility and gentleness, with patience, bearing with one another in love, eager to maintain the unity of the Spirit in the bond of peace. There is one body and one Spirit—just as you were called to the one hope that belongs to your call—one Lord, one faith, one baptism, one God and Father of all, who is over all and through all and in all. EPHESIANS 4:1–6

God created each of us for a specific purpose. We are all unique children of God. He has given each of us passions that we are called to follow in our lives. The initial decision to follow our calling in life is not always an easy one. We worry about the financial impacts, the difficulties in getting started, or numerous other worldly concerns that are a part of our human nature. We need to let go of whatever is holding us back and trust God completely. God will take care of us. That being said, we should always be patient and prayerfully consider our actions before making any dramatic changes in our lives. We need to be sure that they are being done for the right reasons and are consistent with God's plan.

Our main purpose is to accept Jesus Christ as our Lord and Savior, living a life consistent with His teachings. We should share the light and love of Christ with everyone we meet. First and foremost, we need to be defined by our Christian faith. We are not defined by our jobs, our finances, our education, or our race. We are united as one in the body of Christ. We have a responsibility to treat everyone with dignity, respect, patience, and love, seeking peace with all and encouraging others to live as Christ did.

We have a duty to all of the children in our lives. We are called to lead them in our Christian faith. We also need to encourage them to follow their passions and not ours, supporting them in choosing the life God has called them to. We also have a responsibility to make sure that they enjoy their childhood. Make certain that children are not too eager to become adults. Children today are growing up faster than ever. They are exposed to much more than we were as children. Technology, including the Internet, has made information more accessible. Be diligent in restricting and monitoring your child's use of the Internet. Encourage them to be patient and to enjoy being a child.

HARVEST THE FRUIT: Be patient in fulfilling what God is calling you to do in your life. He has given you unique talents and passions that He can use to further His Kingdom. If you are not sure what God's calling is for you, pray and ask Him for direction. Discuss the distinct characteristics you have that make you a special and exceptional child of God. Encourage children to enjoy their childhood and follow their passions in life.

Week 41: Kindness

⁓

Jesus replied, "A man was going down from Jerusalem to Jericho, and he fell among robbers, who stripped him and beat him and departed, leaving him half dead. Now by chance a priest was going down that road, and when he saw him he passed by on the other side. So likewise a Levite, when he came to the place and saw him, passed by on the other side. But a Samaritan, as he journeyed, came to where he was, and when he saw him, he had compassion. He went to him and bound up his wounds, pouring on oil and wine. Then he set him on his own animal and brought him to an inn and took care of him. And the next day he took out two denarii and gave them to the innkeeper, saying, 'Take care of him, and whatever more you spend, I will repay you when I come back.' Which of these three, do you think, proved to be a neighbor to the man who fell among the robbers?" He said, "The one who showed him mercy." And Jesus said to him, "You go, and do likewise." LUKE 10:30–37

The term *Good Samaritan* is still used today to describe someone who shows kindness to a stranger. The parable of the good Samaritan is one of the many parables Jesus used in His teachings. Jesus was being tested by a lawyer when He was asked who our neighbor is according to the Law, which stated you should love your neighbor as yourself. Jesus' response was insightful, groundbreaking, and shocking to the Jewish audience He was speaking to.

Samaritans and Jews did not get along during Jesus' time. They were known to dislike each other. A Levite and a priest both came across a man who was severely beaten and robbed on the road from Jerusalem to Jericho. It was a dangerous area where there was a significant risk of being injured or even killed by thieves. The Levite and priest were Jewish, but they passed by, leaving the man lying on the side of the road. The Samaritan stopped and helped the man, even though it put him in danger. He took the beaten man to an inn and paid for the man's care. The Samaritan showed the man compassion, even though he did not know him, expecting nothing in return for his acts of kindness.

We are called to show compassion and kindness to everyone. Our neighbors in God's eyes are not just our family members, friends, or people who live next to us. We are all children of God. We should treat everyone with love and respect. It will not always be easy to show kindness to everyone, but it is a great way to show others our Christian character. Being willing to help someone in need can have a positive impact on both the person you are helping and on you. Show kindness, and you will receive kindness in return.

HARVEST THE FRUIT: Be a Good Samaritan to someone in need. Discuss the different ways we can show kindness to others. Start by being kind to your loved ones and friends. It will take some effort, but continue to branch out and increase the number of people that you show kindness to. As you continue showing kindness to more and more people, the easier it will become. Kindness multiplies, and soon you will be surrounded by it.

Week 42: Goodness

Repay no one evil for evil, but give thought to do what is honorable in the sight of all. If possible, so far as it depends on you, live peaceably with all. Beloved, never avenge yourselves, but leave it to the wrath of God, for it is written, "Vengeance is mine, I will repay, says the Lord." To the contrary, "if your enemy is hungry, feed him; if he is thirsty, give him something to drink; for by so doing you will heap burning coals on his head." Do not be overcome by evil, but overcome evil with good. ROMANS 12:17–21

We all have people or groups of people in our lives that we don't get along with. It could be an individual who wronged you or a loved one. It could be a group of people who have extremely different beliefs from your own or radical members of another religion that have committed terrible atrocities. Whatever it may be, we need to be careful and mindful of our actions. It is not fair to stereotype a complete group based on the actions of a few people in that group. It is often only a small percentage of the group that commits the radical actions that we too often see throughout the world.

I hope that you don't have anyone in your life that you consider an enemy. Even if you do, we are called to show goodness to everyone. It is part of our human nature to want to get even or hurt someone who has caused us pain. It could be a bully at school, someone who has stolen from us, or someone who has ridiculed us. In all circumstances, we are commanded to do what is honorable to all. We should never repay evil with evil. The best way to overcome evil is with good. If someone wrongs us and we retaliate, it can start a continuous cycle of fighting that goes back and forth. If we repay evil with good, the wrongdoer is more likely to eventually put an end to their behavior. The Bible says that showing goodness is the best response when someone wrongs you. It shows them that you are above their harmful actions and that you are not allowing it to have a negative impact on your life. If we don't provide additional fuel to the fire, it will eventually burn out.

We are called to share the love of God and live peacefully with all. God is our Creator and ultimate judge. He will hold everyone accountable for their actions. If we continuously treat others with love, our reward through Jesus Christ will be beyond our comprehension. It is not the easiest thing to do, but the more we overcome evil with good, the easier it will become. Our actions will also serve as a beacon drawing others to Christ.

HARVEST THE FRUIT: Ask God to give you the strength to overcome evil with good. Pray that you can become a beacon for the hope and love that we have received through Jesus Christ. Be careful of stereotyping an entire group based on the actions of a few. Discuss a time when someone treated you inappropriately and how you reacted. Focus on repaying others who mistreat you with goodness instead of retaliation.

Week 43: Faithfulness

Now before faith came, we were held captive under the law, imprisoned until the coming faith would be revealed. So then, the law was our guardian until Christ came, in order that we might be justified by faith. But now that faith has come, we are no longer under a guardian, for in Christ Jesus you are all sons of God, through faith. For as many of you as were baptized into Christ have put on Christ. There is neither Jew nor Greek, there is neither slave nor free, there is no male and female, for you are all one in Christ Jesus. GALATIANS 3:23–28

Before Jesus Christ was sent to this world to be our Savior, we were held captive under the laws of the Old Testament. The Old Testament contains detailed rules that were to be followed in order to be forgiven of sin and earn salvation. The works of the Law required specific actions to atone for one's transgressions. There were detailed instructions that must be followed in order to earn forgiveness. The rules for the sacrifices that were to be completed varied depending on what the sacrifice was for. The prophets in the Old Testament foretold of the coming of a Savior who would provide salvation to all people who believe in Him.

God sent His Son, Jesus Christ, to be the one and only required sacrifice for the forgiveness of our sins. Christ's death on the cross and resurrection three days later provided the promise of salvation to all who accept Him. Our salvation cannot be earned through our works or through following the Law. Our salvation has been given to us by the grace of God. Whoever believes that Jesus Christ is the

Son of God and that He died on the cross for our sins will be given eternal life. Through Christ's death and resurrection, we too can overcome death. Our faith in Jesus Christ will set us free.

We have been given the gift of everlasting life through Jesus Christ. Jesus paid the ultimate price for our salvation. We need to live our lives worthy of the sacrifice that was paid. We have a responsibility to grow and strengthen our faith during our lives. We should continually gain a better understanding of God. We are called to share the love of Jesus Christ with everyone we meet. We are all brothers and sisters, children of God. In God's eyes, there is no Catholic or Protestant, male or female, young or old, or black or white. We are all one through our faith in Christ.

HARVEST THE FRUIT: Focus on growing your faith in Jesus Christ. Make a commitment to live a life worthy of Christ's sacrifice. Devote yourself to growing and strengthening your relationship with God. Ask God to help you share your faith with the people that He brings into your life. Pray that He will use you to lead others to the salvation we have been given through Jesus Christ.

Week 44: Gentleness

Brothers, if anyone is caught in any transgression, you who are spiritual should restore him in a spirit of gentleness. Keep watch on yourself, lest you too be tempted. Bear one another's burdens, and so fulfill the law of Christ. For if anyone thinks he is something, when he is nothing, he deceives himself. But let each one test his own work, and then his reason to boast will be in himself alone and not in his neighbor. For each will have to bear his own load. One who is taught the word must share all good things with the one who teaches. Do not be deceived: God is not mocked, for whatever one sows, that will he also reap. So then, as we have opportunity, let us do good to everyone, and especially to those who are of the household of faith. GALATIANS 6:1–7, 10

We have all fallen short of the glory of God. We will never be able to live perfect lives as Jesus Christ did. We need to repent and ask God for forgiveness of our sins. We are called to forgive and restore others in their wrongdoings with a spirit of gentleness. Always be polite and humble with our words and actions. Correct others with compassion, not with anger. We have a responsibility to be restrained and kind in all that we do. We cannot make everything about ourselves. We are called to put God first and the needs of others before our own. We should never judge the actions of others. No one will ever measure up to the standards that God has set for us.

We are called to bear one another's burdens. Always be willing to help others when they need assistance. Show gentleness to everyone. Whatever we sow, we will also reap. No one can get through life completely on their own. We need the support of our families, friends, and fellow Christians, people that we can rely on to be there for us when we need them. The relationships that we have help us realize that there are others who have similar experiences to our own. Dedicate your life to being a person others can rely on.

We will never have all of the answers in life. Life can be difficult, but with God's love and the support of others, we can overcome anything. Remember to always be thankful for the blessings that we have been given. We can never forget that the manner God asks us to live is superior to our way. When we submit everything to God, we experience a life that He calls us to live. It is a life that is truly worth living.

HARVEST THE FRUIT: Focus on bearing one another's burdens. Be willing to help others with a spirit of gentleness, compassion, and kindness. Always treat others with respect and humility. Realize that we are all sinners and have fallen short of the glory of God. Make an effort to remove jealousy, anger, and selfishness from your life. Submit everything to God, and live a life worth living.

Week 45: Self-Control

Let no corrupting talk come out of your mouths, but only such as is good for building up, as fits the occasion, that it may give grace to those who hear. And do not grieve the Holy Spirit of God, by whom you were sealed for the day of redemption. Let all bitterness and wrath and anger and clamor and slander be put away from you, along with all malice. Be kind to one another, tenderhearted, forgiving one another, as God in Christ forgave you. EPHESIANS 4:29–32

We need to be in control of our words and actions. What we say and what we do have a large impact on the lives of others. Too often, we are hurtful or insensitive. We attempt to blow other people's candles out to make our light appear brighter. Words and actions are used to ridicule or bully. We speak to others without compassion or kindness. We treat others inappropriately, as if they don't matter. We need to discipline ourselves so that we have a positive influence on others. Through our support, words, and actions, we can help the people in our lives accomplish great things

We should always be slow to speak. We need to carefully consider what we say and what we do. We should be mindful to not retaliate in anger or bitterness. Take time to think about the words we are going to use and the actions we are going to take. Do our initial thoughts coincide with what God would want us to do? Would we want to be treated or spoken to in that manner? We allow the Holy Spirit to guide us when we take some time to think about our words and actions. It shows others that we are different when we think before we act. It allows us to be a witness for our faith in Jesus Christ.

Our words and actions show the world our true character. Does the racist or demeaning joke show others that we are Christians? Do our actions correspond to the teachings of Jesus? It may seem insignificant at the time, but we should always try to have a positive impact on those around us. We are called to be the light of the world. Our words and actions can help bring people out of the darkness. We need to continually let others know that we have been reborn through our acceptance of Jesus Christ. We have accepted the gift of eternal life. We can be an example for others to follow.

HARVEST THE FRUIT: Focus on being in control of your words and actions. Use them to encourage and lift others up. Do not use them as a weapon to tear others down. Use the influence that you have been given to help lead others to Christ. Ask God to give you the discipline to think before you speak or act. Ask Him to guide your words and actions, making them an example for others to follow.

Week 46: Love

For I am sure that neither death nor life, nor angels nor rulers, nor things present nor things to come, nor powers, nor height nor depth, nor anything else in all creation, will be able to separate us from the love of God in Christ Jesus our Lord. ROMANS 8:38–39

What a reassuring and comforting Scripture reading. Nothing can separate us from the love of God in Christ Jesus, our Lord. God was, is, and always will be there for us. His love is greater and more abundant than anything we can comprehend. We can never be separated from God's love. It is more powerful than death. We live in a world where things are fleeting and don't last, but God's love is infinite. If God is for us, who can be against us and what do we have to fear?

God wants us to experience His love for us at all times during our lives. No matter what we go through, we need to know that God is with us. His love for us never fails. It is always easier to feel God's love during times of happiness. When life is going well, we need to make sure that we don't become complacent in our faith. We need to continue growing our relationship with God. Likewise, when we face struggles in life, we need to keep walking in our faith and make sure that we don't turn our focus away from God.

We all experience high points and low points during our lives. Life is full of disappointments and heartaches. We all experience sadness, whether it is from the loss of a loved one, issues with family members, losing a job, or life in general not going the way we would like it to. No matter what we face, we can find comfort in the fact that God is always with us. He will never forsake us. He has a plan for us. Even though we don't always understand His plan, God will never give us more than we can handle. His love is there in the good times, the bad times, and every moment in between.

We were created by God in His image. He loves His creation. We are imperfect and will never measure up to the requirements God has set for us. Thankfully, He sent His Son, Jesus Christ, to take away our sins. Without His ultimate sacrifice, we would be lost.

HARVEST THE FRUIT: Focus on the abundant and never-ending love God has for you. Understand that even though life may feel hopeless at times and that everything is stacked against us, God is always with us. His love will overcome anything we are going through. He is always there to comfort us in our times of need. If you are experiencing difficulties in life, discuss them with your family and friends. Ask them to pray for you. Prayer is the most powerful tool we have. It is a direct communication line to God.

Week 47: Joy

Rejoice in hope, be patient in tribulation, be constant in prayer. Contribute to the needs of the saints and seek to show hospitality. Bless those who persecute you; bless and do not curse them. Rejoice with those who rejoice, weep with those who weep. Live in harmony with one another. Do not be haughty, but associate with the lowly. Never be wise in your own sight. ROMANS 12:12–16

Life is difficult, and it seems to be getting harder all of the time. Whether it is racial injustice, war in the Middle East, or acts of terrorism, it seems like there is more suffering throughout the world every day. The world is very different today from how it was for our parents. It will be very different for our children and their children. It would be easy to say that the world is lost and there is no hope or reason to rejoice. As Christians, we are taught to be patient during difficult times, constantly pray for the world, and rejoice in the hope that we have been given through Jesus Christ.

It is important to have compassion for others. We should sympathize with them when they are facing difficult times or sorrows. We should be happy for others when they have been blessed with good fortune. We are all children of God and should do our best to live in peace with each other. This applies to all people, whether they are Muslim, Hindu, Jewish, or Christian. We were all created by one God who loves us. Our duty as Christians is to share the love, hope, peace, and joy that we have received through Jesus Christ. We have a responsibility to share the good news with others through our words and actions. Jesus taught us that every life has meaning. No life is greater than another.

I am sure you have heard the sayings taken from the Bible that "Pride comes before the fall" and "The meek shall inherit the earth." In all things, we should remain humble, never arrogant or boastful. We are all God's creation, and in His eyes, we are all the same. God has given talents and gifts to each of us. We need to support each other and encourage each other to use our God-given gifts to further His Kingdom. By working with and supporting others, we can make the world a better place for all people. Be joyful for the gifts that you have received and for the gifts that others have been blessed with.

HARVEST THE FRUIT: Focus on keeping a positive attitude. Rejoice in the hope that we have received through Jesus Christ. The week will undoubtedly contain challenges, but through prayer and by placing our trust in God, we can get through any obstacle we face. Show compassion to someone who is having a difficult time or has lost a loved one. Lift them up through positive reinforcement and words of encouragement. Comfort them with the love, peace, hope, and joy we have in Jesus Christ.

Week 48: Peace

Put on then, as God's chosen ones, holy and beloved, compassionate hearts, kindness, humility, meekness, and patience, bearing with one another and, if one has a complaint against another, forgiving each other; as the Lord has forgiven you, so you also must forgive. And above all these put on love, which binds everything together in perfect harmony. And let the peace of Christ rule in your hearts, to which indeed you were called in one body. And be thankful. COLOSSIANS 3:12–15

We are not worthy of our God's love. Fortunately, He is forgiving. God, through His Son Jesus Christ, has taught us all about forgiveness. Jesus took our place and was crucified for our sins. We do not deserve the sacrifice that He gave us, but we should accept it and make the most of it by living Christ-centered lives. As Jesus was dying on the cross, He asked His Father to forgive His persecutors, for they did not know what they were doing. Jesus was able to forgive the people that took His life. Using Christ's example, we also need to forgive those who have wronged us.

We all want others to forgive us when we apologize for trespassing against them. Our apologies need to be sincere and from the heart. We should dedicate ourselves to not making the same mistake again. Apologizing for our actions is never easy, but when we are wrong, we need to admit our mistakes. We also need to be willing to forgive others when they wrong us. We have all been improperly treated by others at some point during our lives. Peace can never be achieved if we don't forgive. We must forgive others and let go of what they have done to us. If we don't, it will grind us down and harden our hearts.

I think you will be pleasantly surprised how good you feel when you sincerely apologize for your actions and when you forgive others. It will give you a feeling of freedom and tranquility. It will also allow you to move forward with your life. Depending on how deeply that person hurt you, forgiveness may help you build a new and stronger relationship with them. Some of the best relationships that we have are built on a foundation of forgiveness. We will continue to wrong others, and others will continue to wrong us. We only have control over our actions. We should strive to correct our behavior to reduce the number of times we need to apologize. Remember to always have a forgiving spirit.

HARVEST THE FRUIT: Think about someone who you need to forgive. Pray to God for the strength to let go of your anger, bitterness, resentment, and pain. Also, think about someone that you need to apologize to. Apologize for what you have done and ask for their forgiveness. You will be blessed with a feeling of tranquility and peace when you forgive and ask for forgiveness.

Week 49: Patience

I thank him who has given me strength, Christ Jesus our Lord, because he judged me faithful, appointing me to his service, though formerly I was a blasphemer, persecutor, and insolent opponent. But I received mercy because I had acted ignorantly in unbelief, and the grace of our Lord overflowed for me with the faith and love that are in Christ Jesus. The saying is trustworthy and deserving of full acceptance, that Christ Jesus came into the world to save sinners, of whom I am the foremost. But I received mercy for this reason, that in me, as the foremost, Jesus Christ might display his perfect patience as an example to those who were to believe in him for eternal life. 1 TIMOTHY 1:12–16

The love that our God has for us makes redemption and salvation through Jesus Christ available to all. We are all sinners and are far from perfect. Mercifully, our God is forgiving and patient. God offers eternal life to anyone who accepts His Son, Jesus Christ, as their Savior. Anyone acting ignorantly in unbelief can be saved through the grace of God by accepting and believing in Jesus Christ. Paul, the author of this week's Scripture reading, is a great illustration of the fact that God never gives up on us.

Before taking the name of Paul, he was known as Saul. Saul was one of the biggest persecutors of Christians shortly following the death of Jesus. Saul sought to destroy the church and its followers. He tormented and imprisoned numerous Christian believers. Saul even approved of the execution of Stephen, a leader of the early Christian church. Even after all Saul had done, God chose him to be one of the foundations for Christianity. Jesus appeared before Saul and asked Saul why he was persecuting Him. Saul was forever changed. Shortly thereafter, he became known as Paul. Paul became one of the most influential supporters of Christianity. God used Paul to grow the Christian church and to continue the ministry of Jesus. Paul authored nearly half of the books of the New Testament. Paul was imprisoned numerous times and was eventually put to death because of his faith.

God uses people in ways which we will never understand. We are all a part of His grand design. He wants us all to reach our full potential. His patience provides salvation to all sinners who repent and place their faith in Jesus Christ. Continually pray for and be a witness to those who have not yet accepted salvation through Jesus. God could use them in extraordinary ways just like He did with Paul.

HARVEST THE FRUIT: Focus on being patient with those who have not yet accepted Jesus Christ. Pray for them and ask the Lord to use you as an instrument to further His Kingdom. Share the love, peace, hope, and patience we have in Jesus Christ with everyone you meet. Read about the conversion of Saul in Acts 9 and Paul's wonderful ministry throughout the book of Acts.

Week 50: Kindness

You have heard that it was said, 'An eye for an eye and a tooth for a tooth.' But I say to you, Do not resist the one who is evil. But if anyone slaps you on the right cheek, turn to him the other also. And if anyone would sue you and take your tunic, let him have your cloak as well. And if anyone forces you to go one mile, go with him two miles. MATTHEW 5:38–41

We all know people who seem to have an endless supply of kindness. They are willing to do anything for the people in their lives. They are always willing to lend a hand when you need help moving something or have a large project to complete. They do things out of the goodness of their heart, without expecting anything in return. They are the first people to show up and the last people to leave. It is important to have people like that in our lives. People that we can count on in any situation. I hope you are blessed to have someone like that in your life. Even more so, I hope you are someone like that.

Retaliation was encouraged under Old Testament law. Exodus 21:24 specifically states "eye for eye, tooth for tooth, hand for hand, foot for foot." Jesus taught that retaliation is not acceptable. Instead, we are to repay evil with kindness. Jesus taught that if we are wronged by someone, we should turn the other cheek. If someone forces you to do something, you should do more than they required of you. This does not mean that we are doormats or that we let people walk all over us. We are called to treat others with a spirit of love, kindness, and compassion in all situations. We should not be keeping score on who has been kind or who has mistreated us. Jesus Christ has paid our debt and the final outcome is already determined.

As the Son of God, Jesus Christ, provided us with the perfect definition of what kindness is. He was willing to give His life for ours. Christ's sacrifice for us was more than we deserved. We will never be able to fully repay Him for what He has done for us. We should start by living our lives to the best of our abilities and as He taught. Sharing love, joy, hope, patience, and kindness with all of His creation. We must always remember that we are to put the needs of others before our own.

HARVEST THE FRUIT: Focus on repaying someone who mistreats you with complete kindness. Be the embodiment of the kindness that God has given to us. If someone asks you for a favor, be willing to go above and beyond their request. As Christians, we are called to continually show kindness to others. Tell the people who are always there for you how much you appreciate them.

Week 51: Goodness

Finally, brothers, pray for us, that the word of the Lord may speed ahead and be honored, as happened among you, and that we may be delivered from wicked and evil men. For not all have faith. But the Lord is faithful. He will establish you and guard you against the evil one. And we have confidence in the Lord about you, that you are doing and will do the things that we command. May the Lord direct your hearts to the love of God and to the steadfastness of Christ. As for you, brothers, do not grow weary in doing good. 2 THESSALONIANS 3:1–5, 13

We should never grow weary in doing good. This doesn't mean we should only do good to our loved ones or the people who have the same beliefs as us. We are commanded to do good to everyone. We can be good to others through our actions and our words. We can also do good to others by praying for them. We pray for our loved ones. We should also pray for the people that we don't have good relationships with. We should pray for those who have not yet accepted Christ. Ask God to use us to lead others to salvation. Prayer is powerful and God is faithful in meeting our needs. Remember that prayers are not always answered in the manner that we believe they should be. We need to trust that God has an active role in our lives and everything works out according to His plan. We don't know exactly what God's plans are, but we can trust that He has great things planned for all of us.

Missionaries play a vital role in sharing the good news and leading others to Christ. They are willing to put themselves and their families in harm's way to share their faith. They travel to places where they could be imprisoned or even killed for their love of God. We should never take their sacrifice for granted. Continually pray for them. Be willing to support their work in whatever ways you can.

It is natural for us to put ourselves in situations that we are comfortable with. We tend to settle into our lives. We don't like to step outside of our comfort zones. We are held to a higher standard as Christians. It is not always easy to go against the crowd. It is hard to stand up for people who are being bullied or ridiculed. It could make us unpopular or targets to be treated badly. We are commanded to treat everyone as the precious children of God that we all are. It is a great testimony of our love for God. Never forget that everything we have is given to us by the grace of God.

HARVEST THE FRUIT: Focus on never growing weary of doing good. Remember that we are all children of God. Everyone deserves to be treated with dignity and respect. Be willing to help others who are being treated unfairly. Ask God to protect those who have answered the call to be His missionaries. Focus on the actions you can take to help lead others to Jesus Christ. It is the greatest gift you can ever provide.

Week 52: Faithfulness

Keep your life free from love of money, and be content with what you have, for he has said, "I will never leave you nor forsake you." So we can confidently say, "The Lord is my helper; I will not fear; what can man do to me?" Remember your leaders, those who spoke to you the word of God. Consider the outcome of their way of life, and imitate their faith. Jesus Christ is the same yesterday and today and forever. HEBREWS 13:5–8

We need to be careful with the things of this world. We should never put our faith in worldly possessions. We need to put our complete faith in our permanent God. Money and the things of this world are not bad in and of themselves. It is all right to be successful and have earthly possessions. However, we need to be cautious that we do not live for the temporary things of this life. The love of money or other worldly things is a sin. The Bible says that we cannot serve two masters, for we will love one and despise the other. Therefore, we cannot serve God and money.

Money can provide us with opportunities to do great things. It can help us provide support to those who are less fortunate. It can be used to help lead others to Christ by providing needed resources to churches, missionaries, and other religious organizations. Money cannot buy us happiness or salvation. It cannot be taken with us when our time on earth is over. We should always use the resources that we have been given to further God's Kingdom and not for our own selfish reasons. We need to remember that everything we have is given to us by the grace of God. We are only stewards of the things that we accumulate during our lives. We do not truly own anything. Everything is God's.

God is the same yesterday, today, and tomorrow. He is the one thing in our lives that will never change. We can count on Him in any and every situation we face. We can be confident that He will never leave or forsake us. God provides us with people and resources that can help us grow in our faith. Likewise, God can use us to lead others to Him. We have a responsibility to share our faith with others when we have the opportunity. Trust in God, and do not be afraid. If God is for us, who can be against us?

HARVEST THE FRUIT: Focus on putting your faith in God and not in material things. If you have a problem relying too heavily on worldly possessions, ask God to help you put your complete reliance on Him. Use the resources that you have been given to help lead others to Jesus Christ. Remember that God is our helper. With Him on our side, we can accomplish anything.